Making Bows

WITH CHILDREN

Making Bows

WULF HEIN

WITH CHILDREN

Schiffer Publishing Ltd

4880 Lower Valley Road • Atglen, PA 19310

Illustration / Photos - Wulf Hein
Layout / Graphics / Cover - Annelie Wagner

All illustrations by the author; illustrations on page 20 and 28 by arrangement with echtzeitMEDIA, Würzburg; illustrations on page 21 and 35 by arrangement with Hase&Igel-Verlag, Garching

Other Schiffer Books on Related Subjects:

The Bow Builder's Book, 978-0-7643-2789-6, $34.95
Bow Accessories, 978-0-7643-3035-3, $34.99
The Bow Builder's Book: European Bow Building from the Stone Age to Today, 2nd Edition, 978-0-7643-4153-3, $34.99
Legends in Archery: Adventurers with Bow and Arrow, 978-0-7643-3575-4, $29.99

Translated by Omicron Language Solutions, LLC
Designed by Mark David Bowyer
Type set in ITC Officina Serif / ITC Officina Sans

ISBN: 978-0-7643-4442-8
Printed in China

Schiffer Books are available at special discounts for bulk purchases for sales promotions or premiums. Special editions, including personalized covers, corporate imprints, and excerpts can be created in large quantities for special needs. For more information contact the publisher.

Published by Schiffer Publishing, Ltd.
4880 Lower Valley Road
Atglen, PA 19310
Phone: (610) 593-1777; Fax: (610) 593-2002
E-mail: Info@schifferbooks.com

For the largest selection of fine reference books on this and related subjects, please visit our website at: **www.schifferbooks.com.**
You may also write for a free catalog.

This book may be purchased from the publisher.
Please try your bookstore first.

We are always looking for people to write books on new and related subjects. If you have an idea for a book, please contact us at: **proposals@schifferbooks.com.**

In Europe, Schiffer books are distributed by
Bushwood Books
6 Marksbury Ave.
Kew Gardens
Surrey TW9 4JF England
Phone: 44 (0) 20 8392 8585; Fax: 44 (0) 20 8392 9876
E-mail: info@bushwoodbooks.co.uk
Website: www.bushwoodbooks.co.uk

For all those who have been asking me for this book for years. And for Dieter Ruths.

Acknowledgments

While you can write a book like this on your own, many people were involved in getting it to lay in front of you now. They have shared their rich treasure of experiences with me in innumerable conversations. They said, "Write that!"

They ironed out my words wherever they were too chaotic. They read, planned, and printed; in short: they made this book possible.

Thus, my heartfelt thanks go out to: Volker Alles, Tobias Barth, Hartmut and Ute Hahn, Angelika Hörnig and her publishing company, Thorsten Kreutzfeld, Axel Küster, Dirk Lornsen, Rieke and Marquardt Lund, Harm Paulsen, Jürgen Junkmanns, Leif Steguweit, the members of archaeoforum.de, and, of course, my family — and everyone else who I may have forgotten or couldn't list since there won't be enough room...

And if a mistake should have found its way in this book somewhere, that, of course, is entirely my doing.

Author's Note: Not just boys love archery, but girls too! Normally I would have always written "male and female archer." However, that would have made reading this book unnecessarily difficult. Therefore, I decided to forego doing that and only used the male form. I hope the ladies will forgive me...

Contents

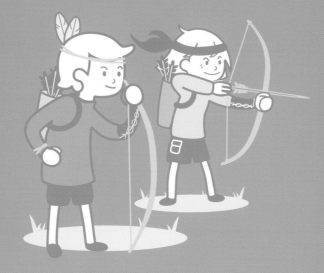

Introduction

Here I will tell you how I came to archery, why I had trouble with my uncle when I was a boy, and what is so wonderful about letting little sticks fly.

At the end of the 1960s, there was neither a Game Boy nor a PlayStation, television had three stations in black and white, and we were allowed to watch *The Sandman*, *Flipper*, and *Bonanza*. Our life was: "Do it yourself outside."

Directly in front of our house there was an old railroad dam, totally overgrown and covered with lots of bushes and trees. Trains hadn't run there for a long time. This is where we went sledding in the winter, and the rest of the year we snuck through the underbrush like our great role models Winnetou and Robin Hood. We wore short leather pants and had scratched up knees from March until October. The others could be cowboys all they wanted, but we were always the Indians...because they had bows and arrows. Well, they were the good guys anyhow. That's what we thought. Just like Robin Hood and his people.

Our **equipment** was homemade. A hazel stick, slightly pointed at the top and bottom, served as the bow. To decorate it, I had peeled the bark off my stick in a spiral and wrapped the handle with packaging twine — it looked great. The bowstring was made of packaging twine, too. It was tied to the bow at the top and bottom. I knew how to tie knots, as my father was a captain and taught me everything you had to know about mooring ropes, ropes, and strings. We made the arrows out of reed, which grew in abundance down by the river. At the tip, we placed half a cork — a condition set by our parents. Anything else would be too dangerous, they warned. Sometimes we had trouble with the feathers since our neighbor didn't have any chickens in his garden, only rabbits. However, with a bit of luck, you could find some by the river or at the city lake where the big swans lived.

We went on the warpath after that, or raided the Sheriff of Nottingham and his henchmen. Those were the kids from Bismarck Street. We never really shot at each other; we just pretended. After all, the cowboys didn't have any real guns either. Even if someone was hit on occasion, no blood was spilled, since the arrows flew *very* slowly due to the corks and the bows being weak. Sometimes we did take off the corks and competed with the reed arrows for a piece of styrofoam. Whoever won got to choose a soccer player trading card from the others. The losers had to give it up. Once I lost two of my best cards on a single afternoon. Not a good day for archery...

One day we visited my uncle in Lübeck. He had just been to sea as a sailor for half a year to earn money. His steamer brought steel to India and picked up wood from Africa for a wood dealer in Hamburg on the way back. Loading the ship took several days, so my uncle had a chance to go ashore and sightsee in Africa; of course, not all of Africa — just the harbor and its surroundings. Together with two other sailors he rented a car and drove around a bit. In a village along the country road there was a store that sold groceries and all sorts of knickknacks, as well as souvenirs for tourists. And here my uncle saw something he just had to have: a bow as tall as a man, made of a heavy, dark wood with three arrows, and a quiver made of a hollowed out tree root. After a bit of haggling he bought all of it together for an — as he thought — appropriate price and took it on board of his ship. At home he hung the bow and arrow on the wall as a souvenir of Africa.

As soon as I entered the room and saw the bow, I started peppering him: "When are we going to go shoot the bow? Uncle Paul, will you go shooting with us? Pleeeaase!! Uncle Paul...!" Finally he gave in, took the equipment off the wall and went down to the river with me and my cousins. I got to carry the bow and proudly ran after the other three. The bow was strung, and finally I could not take it any longer. I put an arrow on the bowstring and pulled. I hadn't planned on shooting! I imagined I was a giant black African chief who was roaming the jungle. I could almost hear the monkeys and the parrots screaming in the trees when it happened.

The bow was indeed made for a grown man and was very hard to draw. For a Northern German pip-squeak, it was much too strong, but I had only pulled the string a tiny bit.... Nevertheless, it slid through my fingers and the arrow zoomed off.

As if in slow motion, I stared after the projectile. The arrow could have flown anywhere, but who did it hit? My cousin Wiebke...in the back of her head. There was a dull hit and Wiebke screamed. At the same moment, my uncle turned to me and yelled: "Have you gone mad?" He raced toward me. I escaped with a slap in the face only, since spanking was already out of fashion back then and my uncle is a kind-hearted man. We ran to my cousin, who cried like a lapdog.

My uncle examined her head and said with relief: "Luckily nothing bad happened!" Wiebke had a bump on her head where the arrow hit — a bump that kept getting bigger, but it didn't bleed. It wasn't a concussion either. For in our family we all have an iron head, as my mother always said. And luckily the arrows from Africa were dull in front and without metal tips.

We all had quite the scare. That was the end of archery, before it ever started. I had to take a loud thunderstorm of rants which I remembered for a long time. Later on, when I was an adult already, my uncle told me that he was very mad at me back then. However, he was even angrier at himself. For even though I had caused havoc with the bow, I was still little and could not see the consequences of my actions. My uncle, on the other hand, had neglected to explain to me in time what you can do with a bow and what you shouldn't do under any circumstances: for example, putting an arrow on the string while walking and pulling on it. If my cousin had turned around in that instant when the arrow went flying towards her, an eye could have been gone!

From that day forward there was no more Winnetou and Robin Hood. I carved a wooden gun and a sword for myself and didn't touch a bow for years.

Not until I was almost twenty did I come to know another guitarist while making music who didn't just pluck the strings on his instrument, but also the strings on his bow. He had a beautiful old fiberglass bow that he still shoots today. I enjoyed visiting him...we often walked through the meadows and forests and shot at rotten tree stumps and bushels of grass or simply let an arrow zoom off into the sky. That was different from the decorated hazel stick and the reeds. A modern sport bow still accurately shoots at fifty yards and could go over two hundred yards. It is incredibly fun to draw a bow, to feel the resistance that it puts up against your muscles, to aim for a brief moment, to let the arrow go, and to follow it with your eyes as it flies toward its goal and hits in the middle of the black. Of course, I missed the first time and was glad if I even hit the target. However, that improved quickly. After a few days of practice, I had gotten the hang of it.

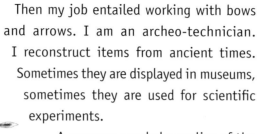

Then my job entailed working with bows and arrows. I am an archeo-technician. I reconstruct items from ancient times. Sometimes they are displayed in museums, sometimes they are used for scientific experiments.

A museum needed a replica of the oldest bow in the world. I researched which one that was, got a small elm trunk, and split it to reconstruct the bow for the exhibit from one half. I turned the other half into a Stone Age bow for myself and made arrows and a quiver to go with it. I still shoot this bow today after twenty years. It is my absolute favorite and works without any problems.

In the meantime, there are more and more archers that hang their plastic covered sports bows on the wall and prefer to shoot a simple wooden bow they built themselves. We gather once a year for a tournament in which only replicas of bows from archeology are permitted. Here winning isn't really the important thing: it's about being there and participating — and I have to tell you, there is hardly anything better than to compete with your

bow on a sunny day in a beautiful landscape against nice people. To get annoyed along with the others when they don't hit the target. To be happy when the arrow hits with a strong "thunk" in the middle of the circle.

To practice concentrating on a point, to feel the resistance when drawing the bow — and to still remain calm and relaxed.

If you, too, are interested in archery and want to build your own bow, then this book is just right for you. Of course, you won't be able to build a perfect superbow with it; there are many specialty books for that. However, they are written for adults.

This book is geared to kids, teenagers, and even adults who may be just starting out and wish to build a simple bow or have been surprised up to now that the homemade bows don't shoot properly or always break right away. You certainly won't be a perfect archer either after reading this book, either. That takes a lot of practice. However, it is meant to help you avoid the standard beginner mistakes.

I recommend first reading it thoroughly from front to back! Even if you follow the instructions for the advanced, you should still read the paragraphs for the simple version, so you completely understand everything BEFORE you get going.

This way, you learn to understand the bow and arrow and how to handle them correctly. Otherwise, you might end up having the same experience I had when I took my first shot — the one that almost ended in disaster. That is why I wrote this book. The bow is a wonderful sporting device, but originally it was used as a deadly weapon. You should always keep that in mind. If you do, then nothing will go wrong and you and your bow will have a lot of fun together.

With this in mind: Welcome to the club!

THIS BOOK DESCRIBES THE CONSTRUCTION OF 2 TYPES OF BOWS:

First is a very simple bow that you can build in a few hours by the campfire without special tools.

I call it **"the bent stick."**

The **bent stick** can be built with a whole school class/scout group on project days or at camps. It is perfect for getting to know archery basics, if you have few or no demands for durability and shooting accuracy. For children 8–12 years old, the bent stick is just right and very well suited to getting familiar with building a bow in the first place.

Here you can gather experience before you dare to tackle a "real" bow; therefore, I recommend this bow model as your first bow.

The other is a simple Stone Age bow, which takes a bit more time, effort, and tools. That turns into the **"Holmegaard Bow."**

Everyone who wants to build a bow following this book, should — depending on age, time, and options — decide on one type.

The **Holmegaard bow** is better suited for the more demanding enthusiasts who are interested in archery and those who are good with their hands and want to build themselves a simple yet durable and precise bow. Young people starting at 12 years old can handle this: e.g., whether it be a project done at home or in school.

Chapter 1

Brief History of the Bow

This chapter tells about bison that were lucky amidst their bad luck, of Stone Age people who were unlucky despite their luck, about hunting, war, and sports — and a man with a green hood. Nobody knows for sure how long we humans have been using bows and arrows. The origin of archery definitely falls into the Stone Age.

Prehistory

The bow and arrow is not the first long-distance weapon of humankind. **As early as 400,000 years ago**, prehistoric people of the type *homoerectus* went hunting near the current city of Braunschweig. They killed wild horses with spears made of fir that have almost the same characteristics as modern competition spears.

Later, about 120,000 years ago, the Neanderthals in today's Niedersachsen (Germany) chased a forest elephant into a swamp and killed him with a lance of yew. In contrast to a thrown spear, a lance is pushed. So the Neanderthals always had to approach their game very closely. Sometimes — if the prey noticed and defended itself — the hunters became the hunted.

Many Neanderthal skeletons that archeologists excavate show injuries like those of rodeo riders — broken bones in the arms, legs, and ribs. That is why our ancestors have always tried to increase the distance between themselves and their prey.

The farther the hunter was from the game, the less dangerous it was for him. After all, an angry mammoth could become very dangerous.

The Ice Age hunters invented the spear thrower about 20,000 years ago. The **spear thrower** is a lever extension with which you could throw light spears for a long distance with great force — an ideal weapon for hunting in an open landscape.

During the Ice Age, it was cold and dry; Europe looked very different then from today. The ground was covered with a grass steppe (tundra). There were hardly any trees and, if there were, they tended to be small. Large herds of reindeer would cross this cold steppe every year on the same paths, and the humans followed them.

At the bottlenecks that reindeer were forced to pass, the hunters lay in ambush...and then spear after spear flew into the herd from a great distance. Afterward, there was the slaughter, and the meat was preserved by drying and smoking it.

Old Stone Age (PALEOLITHIC)

With the end of the Ice Age about 10,000 years ago, the age of the reindeer hunters also ended.

It became warmer in Europe. The forest returned slowly and covered ever larger parts of the land.

The spear thrower was no longer needed because it didn't help the hunter much in the forest. There were too many trees in the way, and there were no more large herds of animals anymore either.

Humans invented the bow — man now had usable wood available in abundance. No one knows how the bow was invented, as there are no videos from back then. Perhaps a hunter was hit in the face by a branch that was let go by the one ahead of him? The oldest evidence for this new weapon stems from the site Stellmoor near Hamburg.

In the 1930s, a large number of arrows made of pine were found here during excavations, along with small flint tips and string notches. Pieces made of pine that could stem from a bow were also found. Unfortunately, all of these artifacts burned during an air raid on Hamburg during World War II. Today only photos remain of those.

Some researchers believe that bow and arrows are significantly older still. From caves in Africa and Spain stem small flint tips that are over 60,000 years old and look like later Stone Age arrow tips. However, they could also have belonged to lightweight spear throwers. And wooden objects unfortunately were not preserved in the cave.

Middle Stone Age (MESOLITHIC)

It looks completely different in Skandinavian moors. If a piece of wood falls into a moor or swamp, it lies under water. There is little oxygen there, so wooden objects barely disintegrate. The microbes are missing...those are tiny animals. They crave wood, hair, and bones, but need oxygen to live. Additionally, the tannic acid in the moor ensures that wood is tanned and thus well preserved. When wooden objects end up in the moor, they can, under the right circumstances, be preserved for millennia.

This is what happened with the oldest known, completely preserved bow in the world. About 8,000 years ago, it fell into a moor on the Danish island of Zealand and remained there until archeologists found it during an excavation.

Named after the site, this type of bow is called **"Holmegaard."** This is one of the types of bows we will build. It was built out of elm wood, a very tough and elastic wood.

In the Middle Stone Age, humans lived as hunters and gatherers. They probably did not live at fixed locations yet, but traveled around in a sufficiently large area. They lived from what nature provided as food. Of course, not like the jungle monkeys that picked bananas.

The Mesolithic hunting devices were very complicated inventions. However, the people had not settled down, so hunting played a large role. Everything that could be eaten was hunted, even large animals.

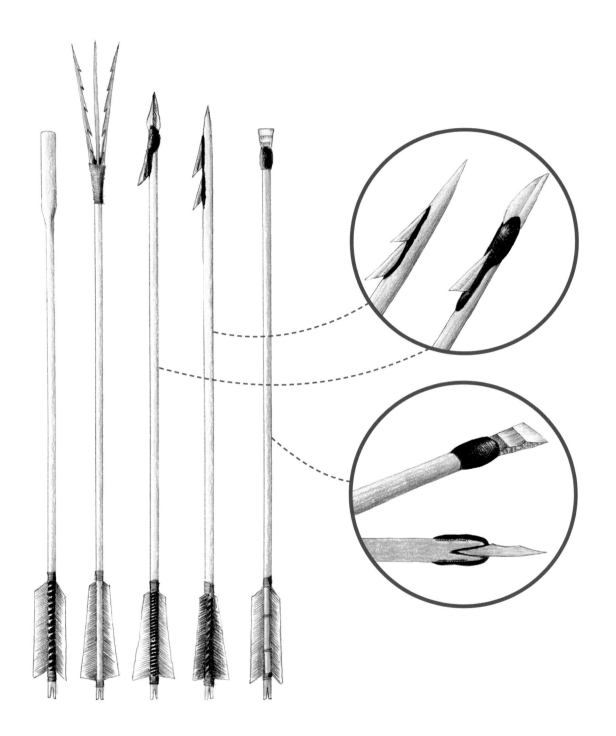

The Stone Age people made the arrows out of the shoots of bushes and fitted them with tiny stone points.

They are also called microliths.

A hunter had various arrows with different arrowheads in his quiver — a special one for every type of game animal.

Sometimes the archeologists can tell from an excavation what life was like thousands of years ago.

Sometimes sites even tell stories:

"The hunters snuck through the underbrush. A twig snapped, nobody spoke. The leader stood still and knelt before a large green pile that was steaming in the sun.

A light breeze drove the odor toward the hunters. The old one smelled it, stood up carefully, and smiled. First he pointed to the sun, then in the direction of the large moor. Then to the hill that stretched all the way to the lake in the direction of the sunrise. Then to the men on his left. The two of them nodded and disappeared in the grass.

The other hunters made their way through the trees. All had hunted together for many summers and communicated without words.

The leader and a boy snuck closer to the moor. The boy had just become a man and was on his first hunt today. Carefully, he peeked around a tree and saw what the old one also discovered in that moment: There was a large aurochs standing in a clearing, eating fresh grass.

"That is meat for everyone! For two moons! Let's just not rush anything now," thought the leader. He lay motionless. The boy copied him. They waited until they heard the quacking of a duck from the hill.

That was the sign: The hunters were in position. The aurochs raised an ear, but continued eating. From the swamp, the cry of a bird sounded. The old hunter placed an arrow onto his elm bow.

The tip had small flint knives glued on, sharp enough to cut through ox skin. The hunter pulled the string back to his chin and raised the bow. He emerged from behind the tree, aimed briefly, and let the arrow zoom from the string.

The ox huffed and turned his head angrily as two additional arrows penetrated his fur, and then two more. He stomped with his front hooves and screamed so loudly that chills ran down the boy's spine. None of the hunters had hit properly, as it was difficult to do so at this distance.

The aurochs lowered his head and ran at the boy. The boy stood still and shot, but the arrow only hit the ox's horn and disappeared, whistling into the bushes. The mad animal headed toward him, and the boy quickly reached in his quiver for a second arrow. He was trembling so much that he couldn't get a hold of one.

But the aurochs stopped because once again several arrows hit his behind. One of those apparently injured him greatly since again the ox screamed, but more from pain than anger.

Before the old hunter could place a third arrow onto his string and find the deadly spot under the shoulder, the ox turned around and ran toward the moor. The leader knew that one of the hunters was waiting there, in a very good shooting position. Nevertheless, he sent a final arrow after the fleeing animal. It only hit the behind, though, where there were already many other ineffective arrows.

The injured aurochs kept racing toward his death. "Come on, shoot!" the leader thought and waited for the hunter at the edge of the swamp to end the hunt with a final shot. However, no bowstring hummed, no arrow zoomed.

The aurochs realized that he had made a big mistake. He tried to turn in place, but it was too late. The soft ground of the moor gave way underneath his hooves. His fore-hooves submerged, the giant body sank sideways and brown moor waters sprayed. The ox attempted to hold his head above water, but the quagmire pulled him further and further into the depth. A short scream, a final bubbling, and then it was over.

The hunters came to the shore, made long faces, and complained. Quietly though, so as not to anger the gods. After a while, the hunter who was supposed to be waiting for the ox there showed up, limping and bleeding. He had stepped into an animal's burrow while sneaking there, sprained his foot, and fallen into a blackberry patch. The thorns had torn his skin everywhere.

had escaped, but only from the hunters. When the men entered camp that evening without a bounty, without a word and depressed, they still did not have to go hungry. The women and children had gathered berries, mushrooms, and roots all day. The one hunter — he had made a makeshift bandage with tinder fungus — did not have any taste for blackberries, though."

8,500 years later: Archeologists found the skeleton of a large aurochs in a moor near Prejlerup, on the Danish island Zealand. Between the bones there were fourteen arrow tips made of flint.

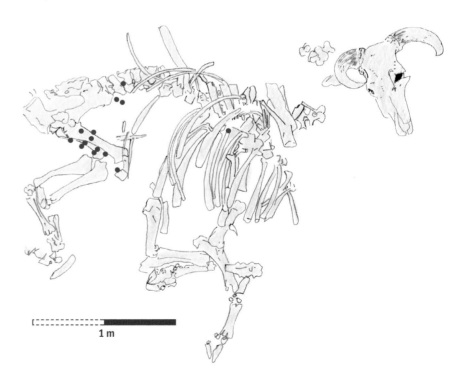

1 m

Despite the pain, he had remained silent, but not silent enough. Startled by the rustling and swearing, a duck had given the warning call and then flown away. The leader had to think the hunter had given the signal.

And thus the plan had failed: The hunters had to watch as the mountain of meat that they had already seen roasting over the campfire disappeared into the moor, in front of their very eyes. The ox

New Stone Age (NEOLITHIC)

Approximately 7,000 years ago, everything changed. From the Southeast other people entered Middle Europe. They traveled, as the ice age hunters before them, along the rivers toward the West and settled everywhere where the ground was fertile. The strangers brought a new way of life with them — they were farmers. They produced their food by raising cattle, working the ground, and planting and harvesting plants. They bred animals and slaughtered when it was necessary.

Hunting was a side activity. The proportion of game bones found at the excavated settlements is very small. The archery bow changed, too. Instead of elm, the Neolithic people often used the wood of the yew. It is extremely elastic and hard, and has been considered one of the best and most popular bow woods since that time period.

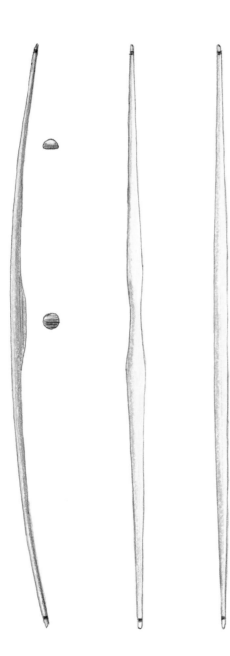

The Neolithic bows are sometimes smaller at the handle. However, they no longer had the pronounced offset limbs of the Holmegaard bow, but rather thinned uniformly from the handle toward the ends. Some of the bows from the Alpine regions also have spoon shaped ends.

The bow no longer served for hunting animals, either.

The farmer has an advantage over the hunter and gatherer: The farmer influences nature and can harvest and eat when he wants to. He keeps his food in his immediate surroundings and can access it.

However, when the cattle is infected by a plague or the harvest dries up, his family will go hungry. When there is nothing left to eat, he can ask his neighbors for help. If the neighbors can't spare anything for him or don't want to, the hunger will kill him. Without unemployment insurance or a social welfare system — that did not exist in the Stone Age — he has to go beg or steal.

And where possessions are concerned, humans have always been very aggressive.

Many fights ended with an arrow tip in the back as early as the Stone Age. Best example: **"Ötzi," the glacier man from Tisenjoch.**

Many theories surround his death 5,300 years ago. Shaman, prospector, shepherd, tribal leader, or sacrifice for the gods — what was he supposed to be? According to current investigations, he died from an arrow tip made of flint that was shot into his back. The tip severed an artery, and the man bled to death on a 3,000-mile-high mountain pass in the Alps. Strangely enough, all of his equipment was still there, too. If he had been murdered up there, the murderer(s) would certainly have taken the very valuable copper axe! It will take a few more decades before the secret of "Ötzi" is solved...if the archeologists can succeed at all.

The estimates are that during the Ice Age 40,000 years ago, about 100,000 people lived in all of Middle Europe. There was room for everyone. Everyone had enough to eat, and there was game in abundance.

In the Neolithic period, that changed: now people, too, were injured with bows and arrows. Over and over again, archeologists uncovered skeletons that had arrow tips buried within them. War came to humans.

To plant grain and keep animals, you needed property. If you owned land, you could produce more food. The population grew, and ground became sparse. And just as the bow and arrow had once increased the distance from the dangerous prey, you now used it to keep your enemies away.

Tribes began to defend their land against strangers. People ruled people.

In Northern Africa and Eurasia, the first advanced civilizations emerged. Cities were built and enormous tombs and temples like the pyramids in Egypt were built.

Repeatedly, individual peoples tried to expand their area of power and attacked their neighbors. Entire armies of fighters attacked one another. Innumerable battles were fought and much blood was spilled. The bow and arrow, once a hunting device, now became a weapon of war.

Aside from the stick bows made of one piece of wood, common up to now, bows made of various materials were now used as well. They are called **composite** bows.

The limbs were laminated; that is, they were put together out of alternating hard and elastic materials like wood, antlers, sinew, horn, and bones, and glued together. This made the bows smaller and easier to handle, so you could shoot them from the back of your horse. The arrows still had great power of penetration since the bows were very strong due to the laminate construction.

That was necessary, too, since people had discovered a new material that would cause great changes: **Metal!**

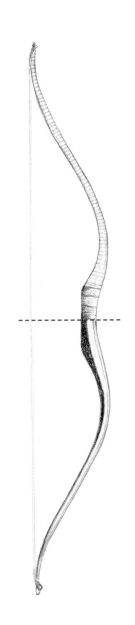

Bronze Age

Though the origin of humankind lies in Africa, after the Ice Age Europeans were influenced greatly by one region that was called the "fertile half moon."

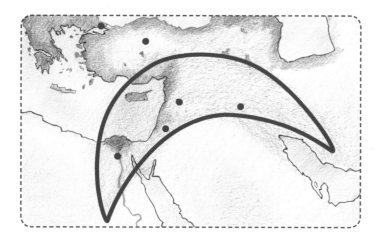

It encompasses Egypt, Israel, Lebanon, Syria, Jordan, and Eastern Turkey, and extends north of the Arab desert to the east, along the rivers Euphrates and Tigris, all the way down to the Persian Gulf.

The Stone Age inhabitants of the "fertile demilune" were good at inventing new things. The first animals were domesticated here as pets or were kept as farm animals, the first types of grain were planted, and the first ceramic pots were shaped.

It was also here that the people realized, sometime more than 8,000 years ago, that certain stones melt if they are heated a lot.

Copper was discovered!

Jewelry, weapons, and household tools all had been previously made of antlers, bones, and flint. Metal now had the advantage, letting you shape things out of it that couldn't be created using organic material. You could turn it into very sharp blades, and if something broke, you could melt it and use it again.

Soon, one of the early blacksmiths discovered that copper was easier to pour if you mixed it with pewter and melted it. This created bronze, a metal with a beautiful golden yellow color that was much harder than pure copper. You could make armor and weapons out of it, equip warriors, create armies out of many warriors, and raid other countries with the armies.

Enameled tile relief from the palace of the Persian king Dareios in Susa (Iran).

Everywhere in the Mediterranean regions and Eurasia, advanced civilizations developed and were constantly fighting with each other. Sumerians, Egyptians, Greeks, and Phoenicians fought for domination using the bow and arrow. This time period provides the first written hints as to their use.

The Greek poet Homer wrote the *Odyssey* in about 700 B.C. It tells the story of Odysseus, prince of Ithaca. He wishes to finally sail home after ten years of war for Troy. However, he has angered the gods and has to wander the seas for another ten years, surviving many adventures during that time. When he finally reaches his native island, he has long been declared dead. In his house, strange men are wasting his wealth and competing to marry his wife Penelope. Finally, an archery tournament is proposed to decide who gets the princess as his wife. Odysseus' bow is brought forth, and with it an arrow is to be shot through the shaft holes of twelve axes set up in a row. However, the suitors don't even succeed at drawing his bow. Odysseus himself participates in the competition, disguised as a pig herder. Of course, the strangers laugh at him, but the prince draws the bow, shoots the arrow through the axes, and chases away everyone who is lingering in his house.

Trojan archer from the Aphea temple of Aegina (Greece). Greek statues weren't always white; sometimes they were colorfully painted.

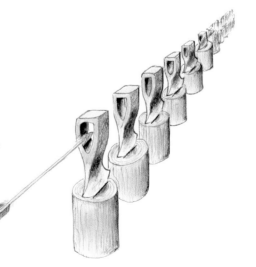

There wasn't just murder and manslaughter during the Bronze Age, though; and bow and arrows weren't just for fighting.

Occasionally game bones are found among the archeological finds. Pictures and traditions tell of hunting excursions.

Also, during the Bronze Age, children and young adults certainly practiced target shooting.

Tomb of Userhat, Thebes, about 1410 B.C. It depicts a nobleman on a hunting wagon, bow in hand.

Bronze-age petroglyphs from Alta (Norway).

Bronze-age arrow tips.

Iron Age

Better is the enemy of good. Thus, the Bronze Age ended, too, because humans discovered an even better metal: **Iron**. It could be turned into steel, and that was harder than anything known up to then.

Now the development of technology speeds up more and more: Over millions of years our stone tools did not significantly change and then humans discovered iron...and soon afterward flew to the moon. A little later? What are a few thousand years anyhow? The principle is the same — whether you let an arrow fly or a rocket. We aren't that far yet though.

The Iron Age is also characterized by wars and power struggles. It was about land ownership, raw materials, and trade routes. Many a king thought his realm wasn't large enough and quickly attacked his neighbor. The neighbor then called his "big brother," and soon help from Rome arrived. This little city state in central Italy first conquered all of Italy with this tactic starting in about 750 B.C. and then expanded over the entire Mediterranean region.

In numerous bloody battles, Rome defeated their competition and finally became a world power. That could only be achieved with a powerful army — and the Roman army was well equipped. During the early empire, the bow and arrow had a fairly limited tactical significance. However, later on, archers were frequently used; sometimes they were even on horseback.

Often the Romans drafted their soldiers in the areas they occupied and then stationed them at the other end of the empire. In the fort of Friedberg in Germany, for example, archers from Syria were on duty. During the time of the emperor Vespasian (69 to 79 A.D.), the first and fourth cohort of Aquitanians secured the Wetterau Mountain region with 1,000 men. I wonder how the soldiers from the Mediterranean fared when they experienced their first winter with ice and snow here?

The Roman bows were copied from the Asian equestrian bows. The Scythians and Sarmatians, horse nomads from the area of the current Ural Mountains, came into contact with the Greeks and Romans in the first millennium B.C. They were feared because of their short but very strong bows. These were reflex composite bows. At the ends of the limbs, so-called siyahs were attached.

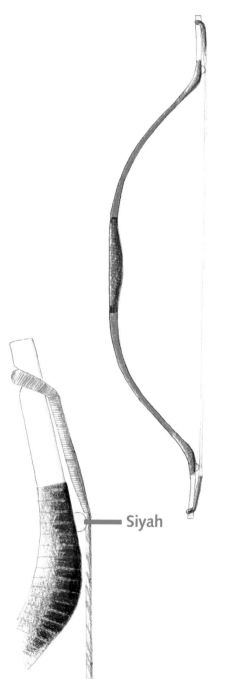

Siyah

Siyahs serve multiple functions:

Simply said, bows gain even more power with siyahs, but are still easy to draw. It accelerates the arrow even more than a simple straight wooden bow. This way the arrow can even penetrate metal body armor. The arrow tips from this time period frequently have three wings.

During the height of its power around 117 A.D., the Roman Empire reached from Scotland to Egypt and the Persian Gulf to Morocco. They ruled the largest part of the world known at the time — and over all of Gaulle as well!

The little village that presented resistance to the Romans was not in France, but rather along the Elbe. The Romans had advanced east up the river around the birth of Christ and probably would have planted fruit trees all the way to Berlin if they hadn't been stopped from doing that by Arminius.

This Germanic prince destroyed the imperial dream of a new Roman province. In the year 9 A.D., he gathered a lot of fighters, lured three Roman legions into an ambush in the forests by Osnabrück, and destroyed them. In this battle as well, the bow and arrow was used, which we can tell from numerous discoveries of arrow tips in the battle area.

It is reported repeatedly that the Teutons despised the bow because they preferred close man-to-man combat. They would have considered the archer who kills with an arrow from a distance a coward. Unfortunately, the authors of these reports have yet to show any proof.

In fact, archeologists have found many Teutonic bows, in particular, during the excavations at Nydam in Denmark. Here the warriors sunk all of the equipment of their defeated enemies in a moor after a battle in about 300 A.D. as a sacrifice to the gods. Among these were thirty-six stick bows made of yew and arrows with iron heads. These bows were characterized by their special tips. They consisted of bones or iron and were probably also used as thrust weapons, similar to a bayonet on a gun. You could clearly tell from the arrows that there were perfectionists and bunglers as far back as 1,700 years ago. Several arrows are very cleanly crafted. Others are made so messily that you have to shudder.

In the south of the Germanic region, bows and arrows were also in use, as the findings at Oberflacht in Southwest Germany show. Here Alemanian warriors had been buried with their bows. These bows have a five-sided cross section in the handle. This is very unusual. They were made of yew and were very powerful.

Middle Ages

The Alamanni belonged to the early Middle Ages that started in 500 A.D. After the fall of the Roman Empire, Europe was divided anew. The Huns headed west from Inner Asia with a mighty army and drove the people ahead of them on their way: Entire peoples were chased from their homeland and were in flight, which is why this epoch is called the time of migration of the people.

The Hun ruler Attila even crossed the Rhine with his armed forces and couldn't be stopped until the Catalaunian fields west of Paris by a Roman army. In this battle as well, bows and arrows were used, especially by the defenders who could cause sensitive losses for the attacking troops.

After the departure of the Huns, small kingdoms developed. Finally, the Merovingians and the Franconians ruled in Middle Europe.

In the meantime, some monks were sitting in a monastery on the small island of Lindisfarne in Northern England, not thinking of anything bad. Suddenly, a series of sails appeared on the horizon. Shortly afterward, the monastery had been robbed of its treasures and burned to the ground. The surviving monks reported to their horrified contemporaries that a wild horde of Northern men had attacked them! The Vikings had entered the stage of world history with the sound of swords.

The Vikings were good archers. Their bows were unique and mostly made of yew. The ends of the limbs were quite thick and reached a bit above the string. They bent *toward* the archer, which was very unusual.

Another unique feature is the attachment of the string. In its unstrung state, it slid on the back of the bow to an inserted string nail. If the bow was strung, the string sat on top in a side mounted string notch. At the bottom it was attached to the bow with a knot. Several bows and arrows have been found at excavations in Haithabu, a trading post of the Vikings at the Northern Coast of Germany. Bows following the Viking method of construction are depicted on a famous tapestry from Bayeux. With its stitched pictures, it tells about the attack of the Vikings on England in the year 1066.

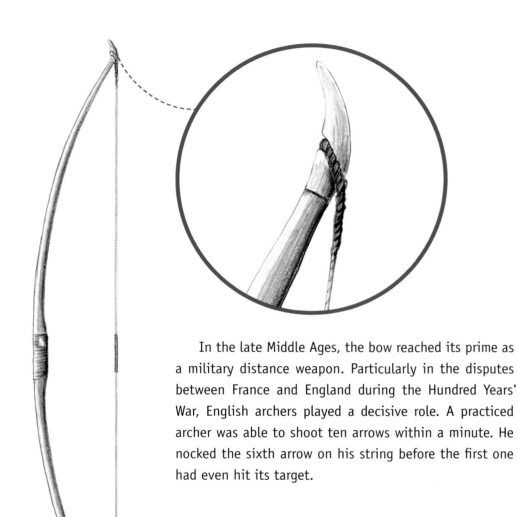

In the late Middle Ages, the bow reached its prime as a military distance weapon. Particularly in the disputes between France and England during the Hundred Years' War, English archers played a decisive role. A practiced archer was able to shoot ten arrows within a minute. He nocked the sixth arrow on his string before the first one had even hit its target.

At the battle of Crécy in the year 1346 in France, 6,000 English archers were supposed to have shot 144,000 arrows at the French within four minutes. The sky was dark from arrows. Many armored French knights suffered a "feathered death."

Bow and arrows were so important to the English that the kings commanded several laws regarding archery.

In 1181, Henry II commanded in the "Assize of arms" that every man whose annual income was 2–5 pounds had to equip himself with a longbow.

In 1369, King Edward III forbade the playing of soccer. Instead of having fun, his subjects were to practice for war instead:

"Hereby We command that every man of healthy body within the city of London use bow and arrows during rest periods and on holidays and learn and practice the art of archery. We also command that upon the penalty of incarceration no one play soccer, handball, shot put, wood or iron throwing, or dedicate himself to cock fights or similar idle games that have no benefit."

The majority of Middle Age war bows were made of yew. That led to yew wood becoming sparse and expensive. Merchants who wanted to export merchandise to Britain had to also import a specific number of bow staves as an additional levy.

During this time period, the yew stands in the mountains of Italy and Spain were so decimated that some of them have still not really recovered. That is why the yew is under nature conservancy in many countries today.

In 1982, the wreck of the *Mary Rose* was salvaged off the English coast near Southampton. This warship sank there in the ocean in 1545. On board, they found 137 yew bows that are so well preserved you could still draw and shoot them today.

Some of the bows were very powerful, with draw weights of more than ninety pounds. When the skeletons of archers from that time period are found, they can be recognized by the changes to their bones that were caused by the constant shooting.

THE ROBIN HOOD SHOT

The most famous archer of all time is and remains **Robin Hood**.

The man with the green hood lived during the Middle Ages as an outlaw in Sherwood Forest. He fought against the Sheriff of Nottingham and rescued Richard the Lionheart. He took from the rich and gave to the poor... that is what the legend tells us.

A real person who actually lived and accomplished all of these heroic actions probably never existed.

The Robin Hood we admire today in movies and on television is a fictitious character. He was created out of several ballads and legends that were sung and retold among the English people between the twelfth and fourteenth centuries. At that time, the simple folk were plundered by the nobility and church down to their last shirt, and they yearned for someone who really paid their tormentors back.

Many of Robin Hood's adventures were composed later, up into the eighteenth century. The most famous one is the so-called "Robin Hood Shot," in which a second arrow splits the first one that is already in the center of the target.

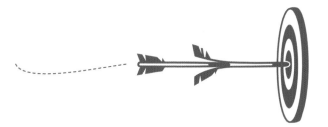

Modern Age

With the invention of gun powder and the development of fire weapons in the Early Modern Age starting in 1500, the bow was slowly pushed aside in wars.

Firearms, such as the musket and arquebus, were much easier to operate and penetrated the heavy plate armor (see illustration on page 35) the knights wore to protect themselves against shooting. The last time long bows were used was during the English Civil War, in the middle of the seventeenth century. There were supposedly individual deployments of archers up to World War II. For the bow has an advantage over most firearms — it is almost soundless.

The Native Americans and other indigenous peoples fought and hunted with the bow much longer, up into the nineteenth century when they, too, were supplied with firearms by the colonists.

However, when pilots discovered an unknown indigenous tribe in the jungles of the Amazon a few years ago, their airplane was shot at with arrows. The Stone Age still hasn't ended!

An African bushman teaches his grandchild archery, 1998.

English ladies of high society at an archery tournament, 19th century.

After the bow disappeared from military use in Europe, it still continued to be used for hunting. Finally, it celebrated a comeback as sport equipment. In the late eighteenth century, tournaments with yew longbows came into vogue in England. Tournament rules were set up, and there have been championships in England and on the East Coast of the United States since the nineteenth century.

Archery also plays a large role in Japan, where it is known as **"Kyūdō," which means "the path of the bow."**

Even here the bow has transformed from a weapon of war into hunting and sports equipment and is often used for the continued self-development of one's personality.

Shooting with bow and arrow is practiced like a ceremony — the point is to be at one's highest concentration, but also be able to let go.

Archery has been an Olympic sport since 1972. In the years 1900, 1904, and 1908, Olympic competitions were already held. Today archers use fiberglass bows that are laminated together out of many layers of wood and plastic fibers.

These modern bows are frequently screwed together out of three pieces: a center piece and two limbs. That is convenient because you can transport the bow more easily and adjust it to your increasing strength.

The last development in the sport of archery led to the so-called "shooting bicycle," the **Compound Bow.** In this model, the string is guided over a system of rolls that decreases the draw weight. A compound bow can be fully drawn and then you can take your time aiming since you barely feel the power of the bow. Once you release the string, it is accelerated a great deal due to the redirecting rolls, and the arrow leaves the bow at **speeds of over 190 mph (300 km/h).**

Many of today's archers prefer shooting a traditional bow, though it does not have to be a Stone Age bow or one from the Middle Ages. However, a traditional bow has no aids, such as rolls, sights, or stabilizers. There are championships all year long in all kinds of classes. I can, of course, be found at the very special tournaments for replicas of prehistoric hunting weapons, where only natural materials are allowed.

In the meantime, hunting with a bow and arrow has become fashionable again, as well, as even bow fishing.

However, to meet at a rendezvous and compete in a tournament, to suffer with the others, and to be happy when a shot succeeds: That is why so many love and appreciate the "bent stick" so much.

Time Table:

Old Stone Age	4 million years – 8,000 B.C.
Middle Stone Age	8,000 – 5,500 B.C.
New Stone Age	5,500 – 3,000 B.C.
Bronze Age	3,000 – 800 B.C.
Iron Age	800 B.C. – 0
Birth of Christ, time change	0
Roman Empire	0 – 375 A.D.
Migration Period	375 – 500
Early Middle Ages	500 – 1,000
High Middle Ages	1,000 – 1,250
Late Middle Ages	1,250 – 1,500
Modern Age	starting 1,500

The years in this table are only approximate values. In Southern Europe, different dates apply than for the north. Even within Germany, the individual epochs start at different times. It depends on the spread of new technologies. When they were using metals such as copper and bronze at Lake Constance, the people at the Baltic Sea were still using flint to make weapons and tools.

Chapter 2

The Basics

In this chapter, we discuss the basics: How does a bow work and why? What do you have to consider and pay attention to before you start building a bow and archery?

How Does a Bow Even Work?

The bow is one of the oldest machines that humans invented.

A bow stores muscle power and releases it when needed. The archer draws the string, which stretches the wood cells on the back of a wooden bow and squeezes those on the belly together. The limbs build up tension because the wood cells want to return to their initial state. (It is similar for plastic and metal. There are no living cells being stretched and squeezed there, but rather the connection of the atoms or molecules with each other).

When the archer releases the string, the limbs relax. The string is drawn toward the bow and with it the arrow. At some point the string stops, as it only has a certain length. Since the arrow is only loosely connected to the string with its nock, it continues to fly, passing the bow in the direction of the target.

In order to hit the target, the arrow needs to fly as straight as possible. For this to happen, the power stored in the limbs has to affect it as uniformly as possible through the string.

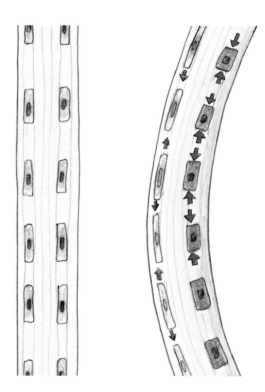

That means: You cannot use just any stick, tie a string to it, and shoot with it. The two limbs of a bow must fit together. More about this in Chapter 6.

The arrows also cannot be made out of just any twigs. They have to be perfectly fitted to the bow that they are shot with.

That is due to the so-called archer's paradox.

This describes the strange behavior of an arrow that is being shot from a bow. In the beginning, it doesn't fly "straight as an arrow" toward the target at all. In reality, it bends around the bow handle, wobbles side-to-side and up and down during the first few yards of its trajectory, and then spirals through the air. The arrow can't go straight through the center of the bow, but has to pass it on the side and bend around it.

Secondly, this is due to the law of inertia in physics: Force is exerted on the nock of an arrow when the string is released. It is long and flexible, though, and heavier in front than in back because of the arrowhead. The head remains at its place for a fraction of a second longer than the end since it is heavy and inert.

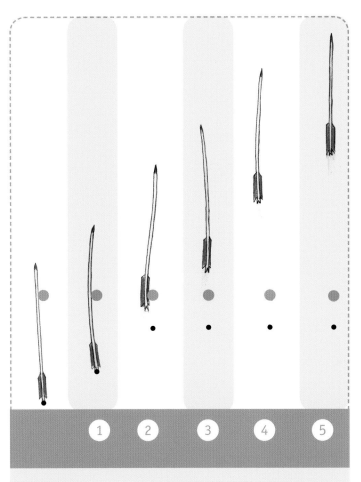

① ② ③ ④ ⑤

Phase 1: When it flies forward, it bends to the other side and back again and, as **Phases 2, 3, and 4** show, swings back and forth during flight. After a few yards, it balances itself enough to fly perfectly straight **(Phase 5)**.

ARROW SPINE AND DRAW WEIGHT

In order to be able to manage these oscillations the shaft of the arrow must have a certain flexibility; this is called "spine".

➡ If it is too flexible, it could break upon release, but will definitely tailspin.

➡ If it is too stiff, it cannot perform the necessary bending and oscillations. It flies who knows where, just not to the target.

The spine value of an arrow, of course, depends on how much draw weight the bow has. And the draw weight of a bow depends on how strong the archer is, how much weight he can draw. Draw weight is measured in English pounds, which is measured in pounds/lbs (1 lb = 453 g). For beginners, it's recommended that they start with a weaker bow. It does you no good to barely be able to draw an 80-pound bow and then be unable to aim with it or properly shoot since the drawing takes so much effort that you start to tremble!

LEFT OR RIGHT HAND?

Before starting with archery, you should clarify whether you want to shoot right or left handed. Right-handed people tend to hold the bow with their left and draw the string with their right hand. For left-handed people, it is the other way around.

There is yet another prerequisite though, and that is the dominant eye. Independent of the right-left orientation of our hands, one of our eyes is the one with which we aim. It is, of course, convenient to draw the arrow underneath that eye. It simplifies aiming. However, it is not required to aim with one eye. More on that in Chapter 10.

You can determine your dominant eye very easily with the following method:

1. Stretch your arms out at eye level in front of you.

2. Form a triangle with your hands as shown in the diagram on this page.

3. Target a faraway object with both eyes.

4. Close the right and left eye alternately. Your dominant eye is the one that still sees the object within the triangle.

5. Or place both hands close to your face — the opening in both hands will be in front of your dominant eye.

If it is the left one, it is likely that you will be able to aim better with the left and also shoot better left-handed than right-handed.

For most people, it is the right eye. If so, you will shoot with the right; that is, your right hand draws the string and the left holds the bow. However, you should pay attention to your instincts as to in which hand the bow feels better.

For example, my dominant eye is the left one. However, I am right-handed and simply started shooting with my right.

In archery, though, you should always have **both of your eyes open** so that you don't lose your sense of the distances and can see around the bow. Therefore, the dominant eye isn't all that important.

Whether right-handed or left-eyed: The main thing is that it feels good and right to you.

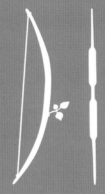

----------------- Chapter 3: -----------------
The Tools

Here you will find out what tools you need for building a bow and where you can get them.

Professional bow builders usually have a large workshop with many devices and machines that they need for their work. I am assuming that most of you do not have that kind of workshop available to you. If you do, all the better. For the others, it depends on which type of bow you want to build. I will offer two types of bows for reconstruction on the next pages:

THE BENT STICK

Very easy simple bow made out of a hazel stick that you can build at a campfire without special tools or much effort.

HOLMEGAARD BOW

Simple flat bow with a handle made out of a sapling, which will require more time and more tools.

The Bent Stick

For the very easy simple bow you need:

- ✓ **Yardstick, pencil**
- ✓ **Saw** (crosscut saw or hacksaw, garden folding saw)
- ✓ **Knife** (sharp sheath knife with a standing blade; no pocket, folding, carpet, or X-acto knife)
- ✓ **Thin wooden stick**, about 32" (80cm) long
- ✓ **Packaging twine**, at least 1/16" (2mm) thick and 63" (1.6m) long
- ✓ **Vegetable oil**, rags

Holmegaard

For a flat bow, you will need a few more tools:

- ✓ **Yardstick**, **pencil**
- ✓ **Straight thin wooden plank**, **protractor**
- ✓ **Saw** (crosscut saw, hacksaw or garden folding saw, jigsaw)
- ✓ **Small hand axe**, **chopping block**, possibly **wood wedges**, and **hammer**
- ✓ **Knife** (sharp sheath knife with a standing blade; no pocket, folding, carpet, or X-acto knife) or even better: **wood plane** and **blade**
- ✓ **Rasp** (not too coarse) and **file**
- ✓ **Sand paper**, 80 grit and 160 grit
- ✓ **Milking grease** or **cooking oil**, **rags**
- ✓ **Thin wooden stick**, about 32" (80cm) long
- ✓ **Roof batten**, one side at least 1-1/2" (4cm) wide and 1 yard (1m) long
- ✓ **10 wood pegs** 5/16" (8mm); 5/16" (8mm) **wood drill**
- ✓ **Glue**
- ✓ **Packaging twine**, at least 1/8" (3mm) thick and 2 yards (1.8m) long
- ✓ **Star twine**

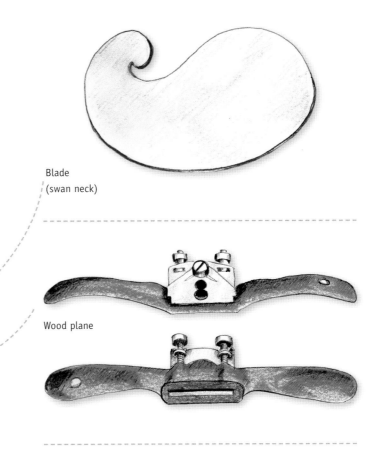

Blade
(swan neck)

Wood plane

A vise and several wide strips of soft wood or thick leather are also very useful.

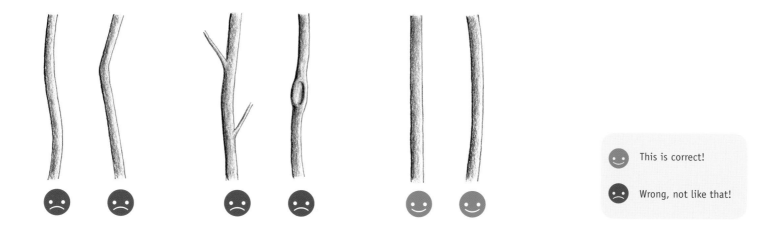

This is correct!

Wrong, not like that!

Some tasks can be completed at home in the kitchen (if you get permission. Mothers — and fathers too — aren't always happy to see you working with wood in the kitchen).

For some steps, you are better off going outside, like when filing the wood due to the dust. That is why summer lends itself to making bows.

The tools are available in most home improvement stores, except for the wood plane and blade, which is not available everywhere. (These can be found on the Internet.)

The plane blade is sharp when you purchase it. However, it does go dull over time. Sharpening it is difficult, even for adults. If you haven't learned how to sharpen it properly, you can easily slip up and hurt yourself badly. When the plane blade becomes dull, visit the neighborhood carpenter and have him explain to you how to sharpen it.

Instead of a plane blade, you can also use a broken piece of glass with a right angle at the fracture. In that case, please wear work gloves.

And if you borrow tools from your parents, please ask them in advance. One day my expensive Japanese precision saw was gone; I only use it for complicated woodwork where 100% accuracy is required. Where did I find it? My son had built a treehouse with his scout buddies and used the saw to cut dirty construction lumber with iron nails in it. Of course, the fine saw was only junk after that.

Safety Notes

When working with sharp tools you should always pay attention to the following:

- **If possible, do not work alone.** If something happens, it is always good if someone else is present that can get help.
- **Always work with the tool away from you.** If you work with a knife towards you, you could slip and injure yourself badly.
- **Only work when you are in a good mood and feel well,** otherwise the stress, impatience, and lack of concentration will quickly make something go wrong.
- **Only work with electrical machines when an adult is there.** Wear ear protection while working.
- **Always have a first aid kit** or at least enough band-aids with you, in case something happens after all.
- **You should wear a dust mask when filing,** and work outdoors, since some wood dust is bad for your health.

**Note: Not all drawings in this book are true to scale.
Always follow the specified measurements!

Chapter 4

The Material

This chapter concerns which wood you can use for a bow, what you need to consider when selecting it and cutting it, and where to get the wood.

Now we have arrived at a very important point, which you should take even more time for than the construction of the bow itself: the selection of the wood.

Just like you cannot turn an old junk car into a race car, you cannot build a good bow out of bad wood.

The Right Point in Time

It is not advisable to immediately run to the nearest bush, cut off a branch, and build a bow in half an hour. Especially not in the middle of the summer. Wood is green in the summer and full of juices. If you bend a bow stick in this condition, then the wood cells are squeezed together and stretched. You can do that up to a certain point. However, if you bend the stick too far, then the soft wood cells burst and tear under the strain. The cell walls collapse and the bow stick either breaks or will no longer bend back into its original shape — then all the work was in vain.

Wood is traditionally cut in the winter, when there is little juice in the tree and the wood needs much less time to dry. Aside from that, you can also see the individual branches or sprouts better when there are no leaves blocking the view. So if you plan to build a bow next summer, then you should obtain the work piece the winter before, giving the wood long enough to dry. The juice evaporates from the cells and the cell walls dry slowly, get harder, and become more stable that way. The wood becomes hard, but maintains its elasticity. The best time is around the first new moon in the new year.

If you have discovered suitable bushes somewhere, try to find out who the owner of the property is and ask him if you can cut some wood. For public parks or streets, the community administration, the landscape office, or the road crew are in charge.

In addition, you should not remove anything from nature during the vegetation period from March 1 to September 30. And of course, you have to respect rules against searching for andcutting sticks in nature preserves! If the wood for your bow is growing in the forest, seek permission from the forest service office in charge. The forest service is usually very helpful if they are asked beforehand. And always be careful near the roads: Never walk along the street, especially not next to a highway! Otherwise you will find yourself mentioned on the radio news in a jiffy and taken home by the police!

The Right Wood

Many who want to build their first bow have heard about the legendary English long bows made of yew and are set on making a bow out of this wood.

I don't recommend that.

First of all, yew is very hard to come by because it hardly grows in open nature anymore, and it is also under nature conservancy.

Secondly, almost all parts of the tree are extremely poisonous.

I RECOMMEND THE FOLLOWING WOOD TYPES:

Maple
(acer sp.)

There are many types of maple we can consider: Norway maple, sycamore maple, and field maple. Maple is not the best wood for a bow, but in an emergency you can use it.

Mountain Ash

(sorbus aucuparia)

Also known as chokeberry. Good wood for a bow, not that easy to get.

Common Ash

(fraxinus excelsior)

Moderate to good wood for a bow,
continues to lose draw weight. Easy to get.

Dogwood

(cornus sanguinea)

Good wood for a bow and for the bent stick as well. Easy to get, plus more suitable for smaller bows.

Hazel
(corylus avellana)

Good wood for a bow, especially for the bent stick. Very easy to get.

Elder

(sambucus nigra)

Good wood for a bow, very hard; not suitable for the bent stick. Easy to get.

Elm

(ulmus sp.)

Very good wood for a bow, but very hard to get. Since the 1920s the normally harmless sapwood bug has infected the tree with a fungus, which destroys the transportation of water within the tree.

Hawthorn

(crataegus)

Good wood for a bow, very hard. Not easy to get.

Locust Tree

(robinia pseudoacacia)

Good wood for a bow, but not
native. On top of that, all of the
sapling wood has to be removed,
which is a job for the advanced.

THE BENT STICK

For the simple bow, we use hazel or dogwood. The wood of both bushes is sufficiently hard and elastic. Also, it grows practically everywhere. The best sticks grow in bushes or hedges, at the edges of streets or brook shores. If the bush is underneath larger trees and doesn't get too much light, you will find nice straight rods in the middle that have grown uniformly thick from bottom to top.

Select one that is particularly straight and has a diameter of 3/4" to 1-1/2" (2-3cm). It should be at least as long as you are tall, best would be if it were 8–12" (20-30cm) longer. If it is bent in one direction, it doesn't matter. It should not have grown to look like a corkscrew, be bent differently on top than on the bottom, or have a sharp bend.

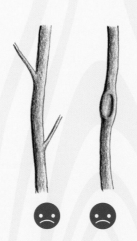

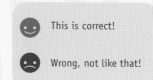

:) This is correct!

:(Wrong, not like that!

Make sure it has no branches or injuries if possible. Take the time to walk around the sprout several times to check it carefully. If everything fits, saw it off. While sawing you should push the shoot slightly away from the cut. Then the saw won't bind. Make sure to saw slowly at the end and to completely cut through the wood with the saw. Otherwise the sprout will break off and then a long splinter could tear off on one side. That should be avoided.

Saw off several shoots in various locations. Then you have a selection and reserve in case something goes wrong.

Once you have cut the shoots, there are two options: Either you continue immediately and shape the hazel stick into a work piece, or you store the wood for a certain amount of time.

If you have the time, you should definitely store the wood as long as possible. Then the wood can dry slowly and your bow will last longer and shoot better. It has been said that wood should dry for one year for each 1/2" (1cm) in thickness. Of course, you want to go out immediately with your bow and arrow. Thus let's agree on a median. If you harvested the wood in the winter, you can build a good

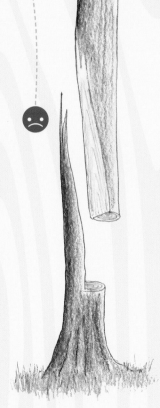

bow from it in the summer. You should invest that much pre-planning time. The completed bow will reward you.

Very important: Brush the two cut surfaces where you sawed off the shoot with glue. By doing this you prevent the juice from evaporating too fast at the so-called end grain, where the cells are laying bare. The result would be that the empty wood cells shrink and at some time the wooden rod tears apart in the middle. As Murphy would have it, the wood always tears where you can't use it.

Apply glue and let it dry. Store the wood outside if possible, in a shady, dry location with lots of wind: Under a projecting roof, on the balcony, or in a shed.

Then it's time to wait. Time enough to continue reading this book. Or other books. Or to obtain feathers for the arrows...

The drying can be sped up if you bring the bow into a heated room after one or two months outside and place it under the bed or on top of the dresser — but never near the heater. Before you construct a bow out of the wood, it has to go outside one more time for a few weeks. If you are too impatient during the drying process, the wood will become unusable...and then you will have to wait another entire year.

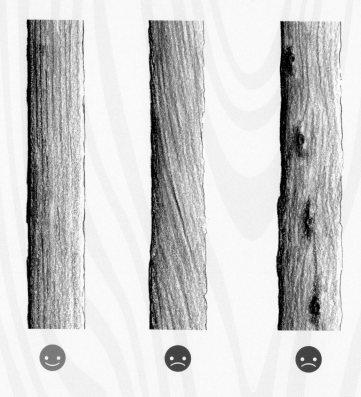

HOLMEGAARD BOW

For the flat bow, a thin hazel sprout is not enough. You need a sapling of at least 1-1/2" (4cm), more likely 2 to 2-1/2" (5-6cm) diameter. While you can use hazel, I would recommend ash, dogwood, or elder.

You proceed as described in the Bent Stick section in making your selection, but you should pay attention to a few more things. Nice straight saplings grow at the edges of forests, on clearings, in hedges, bushes, and at the shores of rivers and creeks. Select a nice one and take your time.

Don't just pay attention to straight and flawless growth, but also to the bark.

Does it run in straight and vertical lines along the trunk? Or does it wind in a spiral around it? Then leave the tree standing, for it has spiral growth. During its growth the lighting conditions changed and the tree adjusted toward the sun over and over. Its wood is unsuitable since the bow you would build from it looks like an airplane propeller and doesn't shoot.

Spiral growth can be detected by the bark and sometimes on small dead twigs that show up as a spiral line on the periderm.

When you have found a suitable sapling — straight and evenly grown, without branches, at least as long as you are tall — then find out who it belongs to and ask if you can cut it down. Only then do you chop it down and take it with you.

One of my friends once took three nice saplings from a wood pile at a highway rest area. He was caught and charged with theft. He could only save himself by providing the employees of the highway maintenance department with a free workshop in bow building.

Another friend wanted to chop down a 20-foot-tall (six meters) elm tree on the highway at night and had almost sawn it off. The tree turned, though, and fell across the driving lane. At the last second, he succeeded at pulling the trunk off the street before a car crashed into it, but then he had to throw up from the effort. His whole car was dirty, and he ended up with several painful torn muscle fibers in his arms and legs.

You should definitely do without those kinds of adventures! For there is another way: "Honesty goes a long way!" After an evening trip to the movies in town, I discovered a beautiful yew and was tempted to simply steal it under the protection of darkness. I thought better of it, though, and called the city gardener the next morning and asked. They said: "No, unfortunately, you cannot have that tree. It has been standing there for a long time and it works

there. However, by the preschool on XYZ Street, all yews have to be cut down — you can pick those up." Asking is always advantageous and protects you from unwise and hasty foolishness.

If you chop down a really small tree, you should take along an adult or at least a friend who can help. Make sure the tree doesn't fall on anything that it could ruin. Even a small tree a few meters tall weighs quite a bit. In particular, pay attention that it doesn't fall on your head!

Once the sapling is at your home, carefully examine it. If it is thicker than 2-1/2" (6cm), then you should split it. Alternatively, you can cut the working material out of the trunk with an axe. **Splitting it has several benefits:** You can tell immediately if the tree has spiral growth and the wood dries more quickly.

Beforehand, though, you have to decide which part of the trunk is to become the bow. For this, place it on the ground and carefully view along the trunk. Does it have a side that is bent inward a bit (that is called "concave")? Take this side. (More about this on page 84.)

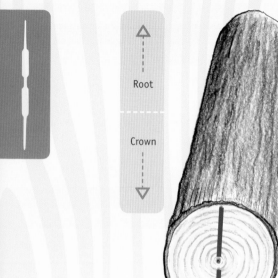

Root

Crown

Good side (left)   Pith

Splitting is easiest this way: "You split as the bird shits" is an old rule. So from the crown to the root, from the top to the bottom. Mark on the top cutting area where you want to cut the trunk in half, so the desired side is split off.

The line has to run through the pith, which isn't always in the middle! However, only from here can the wood be split easily.

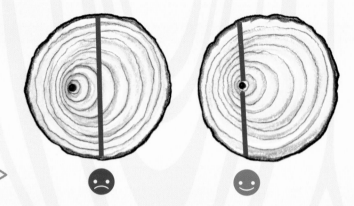

Lean the trunk with the bottom cutting surface against a wall or a large rock/concrete base. It should be able to take some force — you don't want to tear up your Grandma's nice natural stone wall.

Place the axe with its blade onto the pencil mark and hit its neck with a hammer.

Normally the tree will now split into two halves. Sometimes you have to help it along. You can either continue hitting the neck of the axe or use a wooden wedge as an aid. Push it sideways into the split and carefully hit it. Watch out for your feet!

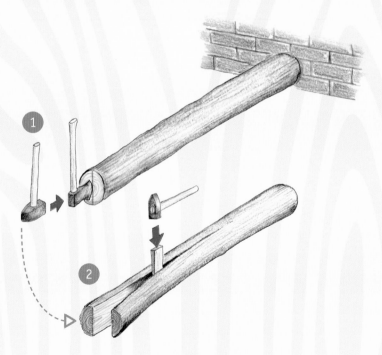

Once the sapling is split, you can easily tell whether it had spiral growth: If the splitting surfaces aren't parallel at the ends but are at an angle to each other, then you got a "propeller." Unfortunately, you can only turn it into fire wood, but then at least the work wasn't totally in vain — as it was for me when I received sixty yew trunks as a gift from the administration of a large cemetery. The cemetery employees had already cut them and piled them in front of the entrance gate for me. It was a giant effort, but I took them all home and was happy every day about the pile of bow wood.

After a few days, I had time and began splitting them. By evening, I had produced — with a lot of noise, sweat, and muscle power — about one hundred completely spiraled propellers. Only ten saplings were usable. I didn't want to burn the wood since, as we know, it is very poisonous. So, with a heavy heart, I took it back to the cemetery and disposed of it there. I was mostly saddened for the gardeners who had just wanted to do me a favor.

If everything went perfectly, you now have two trunk halves that have remained straight. You already chose the better one earlier, which you should have marked on the forehead (top) side with an "A" and wrote down the date

and location where you chopped it down. Now seal the cutting surface with glue and store the stick as described previously. Through the splitting surface and the bark, the wood can now uniformly and slowly release its humidity into the air.

Chapter 5

The Bow Stick

You will need a yardstick, paper, and pencil. You will learn how to draw your bow and discover how you can cut the raw shape out of wood.

Now, after all those preparations, we have finally arrived at the real construction of the bow. However, first you have to determine how your bow should be shaped.

Some say a bow should be as long as the one who will shoot it. That does not apply to every situation though, since a long bow can quickly get caught on a branch in the forest.

A short bow is very prone to mistakes in posture and release.

I make my bows so they reach the tip of my nose, since I don't shoot from the back of a horse or from a narrow canoe.

So measure the distance from the ground to the tip of your nose and add 1-1/2" (3cm). That is the length of your bow.

The extra inches are meant as protection during the work process. While working on a bow limb, you frequently have to set it on one end, either on the ground or a chopping block. This crushes the wood, causing it to de-fiber and become unattractive. You keep the 3/4" (1.5cm) on the top and at the bottom of the stick until the bow stave is done all the way around and no more stress is expected at the ends. Only then should you saw them off.

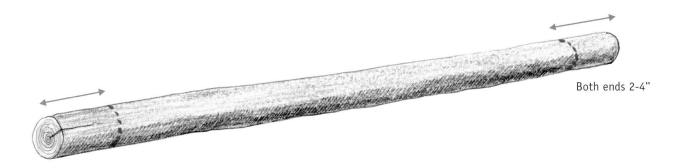

Both ends 2-4"

THE BENT STICK

You can draw the measured distance plus 1-1/2" (3cm) onto the stick now. Don't place the yardstick at one end of the wood, but 2–4" (5-10cm) away from it, so you can later saw off these 2 to 4 inches. Sometimes the wood will split at the cut, and we cannot use split wood on the bow. Once you have drawn the measurement onto it, cut the stick to length.

You can leave the bark on the bow. If you wish to decorate it, you can carve it off at a few places. For example, you can peel a spiral off all the way around, as I did as a small boy with my first bow. If you want to remove the bark, please continue reading on the next page.

Measure the length of the wooden stick and divide it in half — now you have the middle of the bow.

Now determine which should be the bottom and the top of your bow. It is best to keep it the way the stick grew. Whatever was at the bottom in the forest remains at the bottom.

Measure the width of your hand (without the thumb). This measurement is for the handle. Add 3/4" (2cm) and mark the handle, starting in the middle toward the bottom.

The 3/4" (2cm) remain above the middle of the bow. This part of the bow will not be altered anymore.

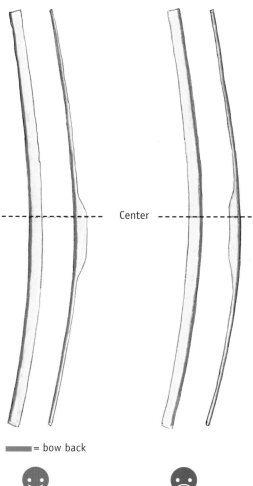

1/2"

Center — 3/4"
Handle

1/2"

Now you can start on the limbs. For this determines what will be the back and the belly of the bow.

If the bow stick grew perfectly straight and uniformly, you can carve it whichever way you please.

If the stick is slightly bent, use the side that is bent inward (concave) as the back. This makes the bow stronger. It is not pre-bent toward the archer, but away from him. This causes it to build up more tension.

You can use the side that is bent outward (convex) instead; however, the bow won't be as strong then.

Center

█ = bow back

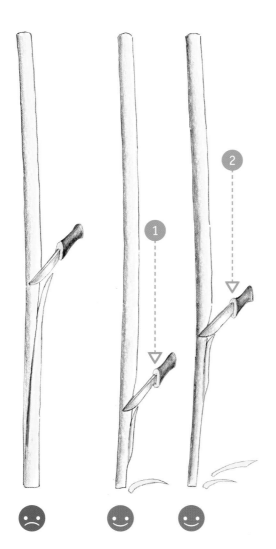

Now you can start removing the material from the belly. You need the carving knife for this. Always carve from the handle toward the tip of the limb. Start at the tip of the limb and slowly and carefully work your way upward toward the handle. This way you avoid having a large splinter break off and your bow becoming too thin.

Always only carve off thin shavings. Be sure to always work with the knife headed away from you, never towards you! Make sure the surfaces that you carved are in one plane. If they tilt, then one limb will later shoot toward the left and the other toward the right.

Remove at most one-third of the diameter of the stick and then bend the bow once again as described above. Now it will certainly bend more easily already. Make sure you don't bend the bow too far at this stage, though. You have to slowly get it used to it or the wood cells collapse and your bow loses its tensioning force.

Use your instinct to remove more wood until the bow can be bent reasonably easy, and then give the wood another break of several days for drying.

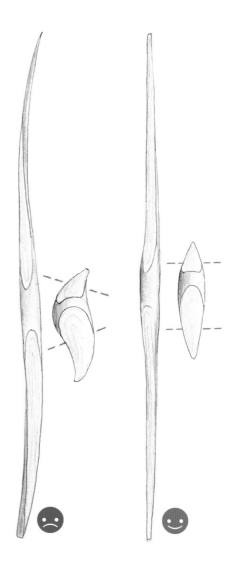

For the Holmegaard bow, you chopped down a small sapling, split it, and dried it. Now the bark needs to be removed. You have to work very carefully there. The wood is directly beneath the bark and the outermost annual ring must not be damaged. Otherwise, a weak spot develops exactly where the bow is subjected to the most burden during the draw. The bow would break at precisely this spot.

Now, take the sharp knife and begin very carefully peeling the bark off the wood at one end. At some point you will see the wood peeking through the final thin layer of bark. At this point, do not cut any deeper, but remove the bark using this method along the entire length of the bow. Next, place the knife, or even better a scraper, vertically onto the wood and carefully scrape the remaining bark fibers off. Always be careful not to damage the outermost layer of wood.

Next, smooth out the splitting surface with the axe. Only remove wood fibers that are sticking out — don't penetrate the wood too deeply.

Our stave is definitely still too thick. You should probably try this:

Place (as a right-handed person) the bottom end of the stick against your right inner foot. With your left hand grab the middle of the stick and bend the upper end toward you. The stick will be hard to bend.

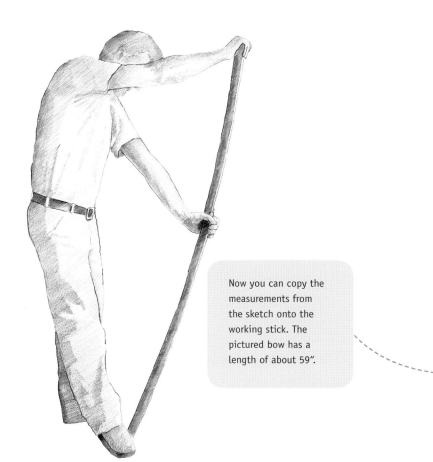

Now you can copy the measurements from the sketch onto the working stick. The pictured bow has a length of about 59".

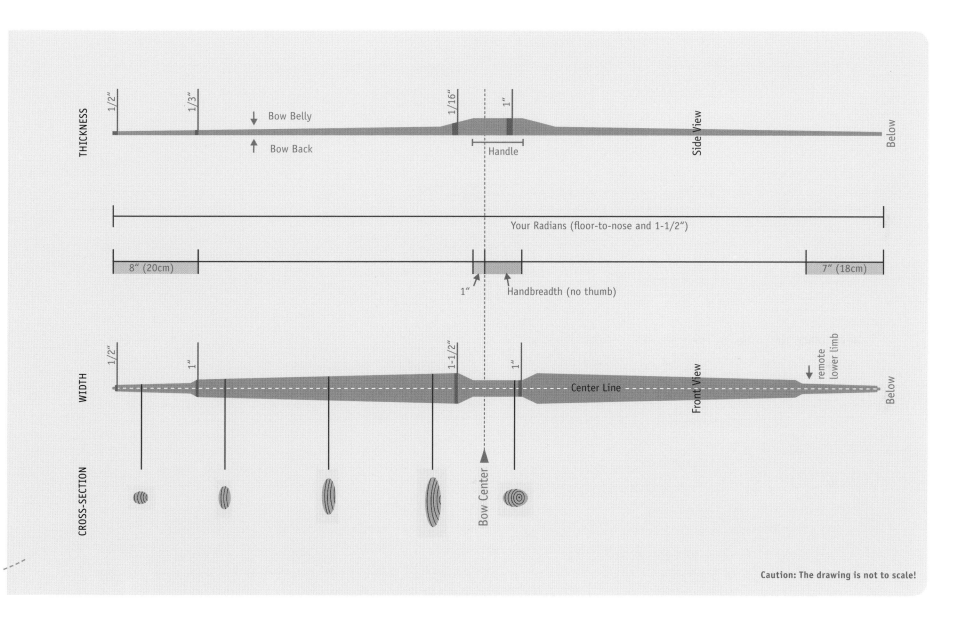

THICKNESS

1/2"

1/3"

↓ Bow Belly

1/16"

1"

↑ Bow Back

Handle

Side View

Below

Your Radians (floor-to-nose and 1-1/2")

8" (20cm)

1"

Handbreadth (no thumb)

7" (18cm)

WIDTH

1/2"

1"

1-1/2"

1"

Center Line

remote lower limb

Front View

Below

Bow Center

CROSS-SECTION

Caution: The drawing is not to scale!

Mark the middle on the back of the bow, so you always know where it is. A lot of wood will be removed now, so it is easy to lose perspective.

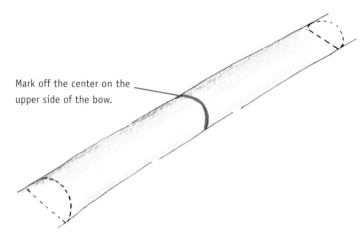

Mark off the center on the upper side of the bow.

In our model, the bottom limb is a bit shorter than the top one. The handle is not in the middle of the bow, but below it since the arrow is supposed to fly through the middle of the bow. Since the bottom limb is shorter, it gets more of a workout. It has to bend just as much as the top limb, but within a shorter span.

Therefore you should inspect your sapling carefully once more: Can you see ingrown branches or small irregularities in growth anywhere on the stick? If so, try to place these weak spots on the upper limb since it is subjected to less tension.

Small branches are generally not a problem if they are located in the middle of the back of the bow or close to it.

They are only disruptive if they are at the edge of the limb and cut only on one side. If that's the case, then the tension in the limb may not distribute itself properly at this weak spot and the bow might break.

So pay attention while sketching that you aren't cutting any branches. Since you are drawing on the future inside of the bow, you can only estimate whether you will cut into a branch. While planning the front view of the bow, you have to carefully pay attention to the branches on the back of the bow. If you get close to a branch, you are better off leaving some wood around it. Use the long slat of wood for drawing.

First transfer the **width measurements** from the sketch onto the belly of the **bow**. Again, verify that the wood grew 100% straight. If the sapling did not grow perfectly straight, you should take that into account.

If the working stick has a slight bend, then the outline of the bow should follow this bend. It is easiest to recognize this on the pith and the annual rings.

Start by marking the **center line**. It should follow the pith. From the center line, mark the width measurements.

On the sketch, the center line is marked straight on the left-hand side. **That is wrong!**
The annual rings are then severed at the edge, which creates weak spots.

On the right it is done correctly:
The center line follows the pith — that makes the front view of the bow a bit snakelike, but that doesn't matter as long as the bow is straight over its entire length.

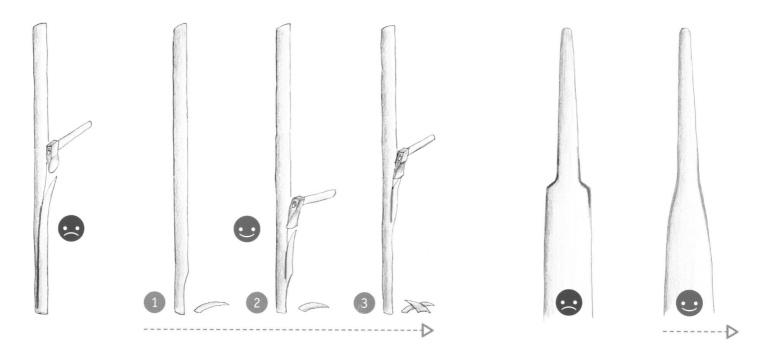

Now you can start working on the front view (back) of the bow. Set the sapling on the chopping block and use the hand hatchet to chop away wood from the sides of the bow. Start on the bottom at the tip of the limb each time and work your way up slowly and carefully toward the handle.

Hold the bow stick so that you can always see the pencil markings well. It is very important that the hatchet is sharp. It's even more important to work carefully and with forethought. A careless and overly strong hit with the hatchet can cause the blade to penetrate far into the wood

and a large splinter to separate or the limb to split...then you can only use the bow stick for the oven!

Work your way as closely as possible toward the pencil markings, but not beyond them. Only remove very fine shavings. Watch your hands and legs when working with the hatchet.

For detailed work, you should use the knife and carve right up to the pencil line. Pay particular attention to making the transitions from the handle to the limbs and the limbs to the offset limb tips smooth.

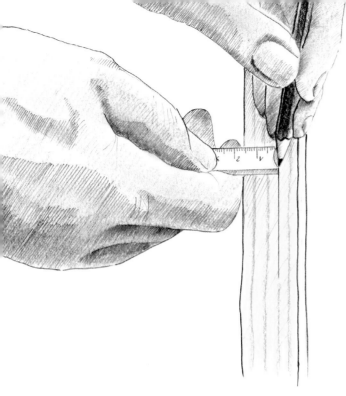

When the front view of the bow is finished to this point, transfer the thickness measurements onto its sides. You can use the yardstick for marking it, as shown on the sketch.

Your pointer finger forms the border on the back of the bow. The yardstick extends beyond the edge of the bow as far as the measurements on the sketch specify (page 87).

This way you ensure that the outline always follows the back of the bow, which is important since no wood grows perfectly. If you use the yardstick as your border, the working stick will always be uniformly thick, even when the wood on the back has small waves. If you don't draw the pencil line parallel to the back of the bow, the stick could possibly be a bit thicker here and a bit thinner there when you carve it. The thin spots would be weaker than the thick ones, and that is exactly where the bow might break later on.

Now you can remove material from the belly. Here, too, you should always work from the bottom towards the top and with care since wood frequently grows unpredictably. Especially when working on the front of the bow, it is possible that you succeed at completing a small piece following the fibers and are headed across it on the next four inches (10cm). Only remove very thin shavings with the hatchet. Always make sure as above to only work up to the pencil mark and not beyond it. You are better off using the knife for the detailed work. The handle should fade out into the limbs very smoothly.

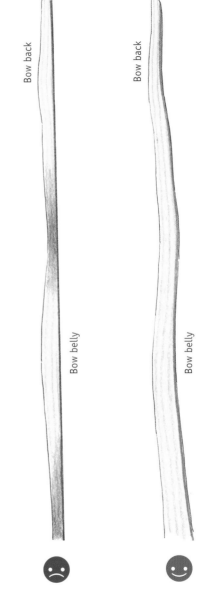

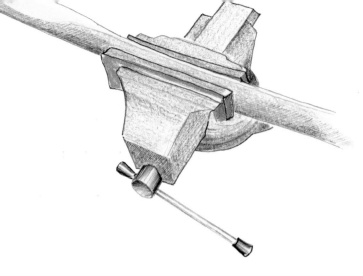

Now you have to shape the handle area. For this you should attach the bow by one of its limbs to the vise.

Make sure you place the soft wood or leather strips between the metal cheeks of the vise and the limb, so the bow's wood does not get squashed. If no vise is available, you can also attach the bow with a clamp (caution: always place soft wood in between) to the work bench or to a table. As a last resort, someone else can hold it.

Finish the handle with the plane and the file. **Here too, only go up to the pencil mark and use the tools along the length:** Don't just rub energetically on the wood with the middle. That takes effort and only wears out the middle of the tool, which would not be economical.

"The whole plane is paid for!" is what my master always said. Try to create as smooth a surface as possible at the end that you don't have to file much. When the handle fits your hand well, you make a small groove on the side of the handle on the left-hand side (as a right-handed person) where the middle is marked on the back of the bow, either with the knife or the file. This will be the point where your arrow passes. Is there enough room above it for the arrow if your fist encloses the bow below the notch? If not, you have to work there a bit more, but on both sides. If you shoot with the left, then the mark is drawn on the right side of the bow.

Upper tip

Bow Center

Lower tip

Notch

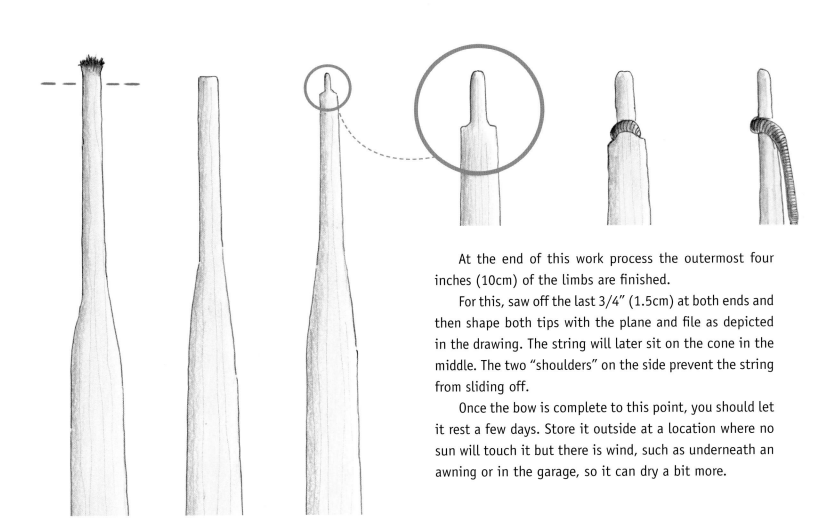

At the end of this work process the outermost four inches (10cm) of the limbs are finished.

For this, saw off the last 3/4" (1.5cm) at both ends and then shape both tips with the plane and file as depicted in the drawing. The string will later sit on the cone in the middle. The two "shoulders" on the side prevent the string from sliding off.

Once the bow is complete to this point, you should let it rest a few days. Store it outside at a location where no sun will touch it but there is wind, such as underneath an awning or in the garage, so it can dry a bit more.

Chapter 6

Tillering

Now it gets a bit complicated. This chapter concerns strange but important things, like the tiller stick, the bow profile, and the draw length.

The raw shape of your bow is now finished. Can you bend it yet? Depending on the type of wood and the thickness, it is probably already possible but the bow is unlikely to bend uniformly. However, it needs to, so it doesn't break and shoots cleanly. For this the curvature of the limbs needs to be adjusted to each other. This process is called "tillering".

THE BENT STICK

Here tillering is quite easy. However, first we have to complete the bow to the point where it can hold a string. For this, sharpen the tips of the limbs as drawn on the sketch. Now the string can rest on the tips without sliding off.

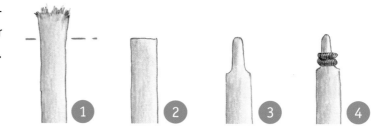

You do still need a test string though. Use a piece of strong cord for this that is at least 1/16" (2mm) thick, and tie a knot at the upper end of the bow. (Follow the sketch).

This knot, the bowline knot, has the advantage of holding well. However, it is very easy to untie again, no matter how much it was tightened. The loop of the knot should fit tightly around the cone of the limb tip.

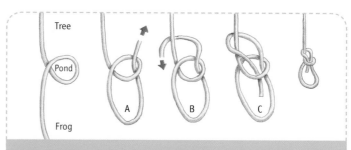

There is a memory aid for the bowline knot:
The frog comes out of the pond **(A)**, runs around the tree **(B)**, and jumps back into the pond **(C)**. The loop forms the pond, the upper long end of the cord is the tree, and the bottom short end is the frog.

CLOVE HITCH

Now, set the bow on the ground with that end and put the other end of the string around the limb tip that is now pointing up, as seen on the sketch (left). Bend the bow far enough for your hand to fit between the bow and the string and pull the string tight.

Then tie the free string end to the bow as shown on the sketch above. This knot is called a clove hitch. Its advantage is that it holds well and can be adjusted.

Check again whether your hand still fits between the handle and the string. If not, loosen the clove hitch and pull at the cord end until the distance is correct and then tighten it again.

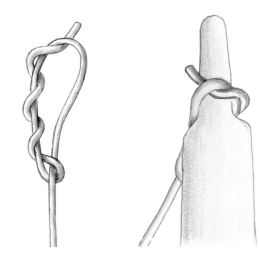

TIMBER HITCH

You can also use a timber hitch or bowyer's knot. However, make sure the loose end is looped around the string in such a way that it is clamped between the string and the bow. Otherwise the knot will unwind.

Now grab the bow by the handle and hold it flat in front of you. Then carefully pull on the string, about 8–12" (20-30cm).

You can measure the draw by marking a thin stick that is 28–31" (70-80cm) long every two inches (5cm) and writing down the measurement.

Place the stick with one end on the bow by the handle and hold the other end, where the markings start, between two fingers of your shooting hand when you pull on the string. Then you can read off the draw at the front of the bow.

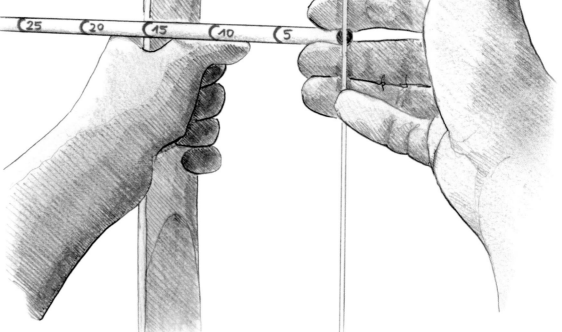

What does the bow look like now? How does it bend? If you are lucky and have done good work so far, then both limbs bend uniformly now. The back of the bow almost forms a circle **(A)**.

More likely, one of the limbs is a bit stiffer — it bends less than the other one **(B)**.

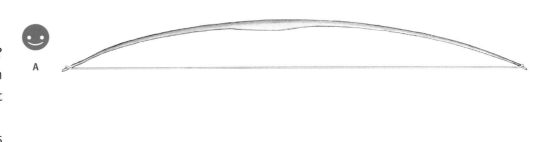

A

B

You have to balance that out. Remove some wood from the belly side of the stiffer limb using the knife blade. You can do this by carving or shaving. When carving, be very careful: You must only remove very thin layers at a time. Thus it is better to use the knife blade for shaving, as shown in the sketch (left).

Draw the bow once again but again only 8–12" (20-30cm). We don't want to strain the bow right away. You have to get it used to what it is supposed to do from now on very slowly: Store energy and release it uniformly. If you were to draw the bow further at this stage, the wood cells on the belly would get clinched too fast and those on the back of the bow would get stretched too fast. The bow would lose its tension or even break.

So it is important: At first only draw the bow a little, and let the tension increase slowly from draw to draw!

Also very important: Once you have drawn the bow, never just let the string go when there is no arrow on the bow. Without the weight of the arrow, the bow shoots "empty"; it is burdened incorrectly and could break...so always hold onto the string and guide it back to the bow slowly.

Now you have removed some wood from the belly — what is the bow doing now? Is it bending more evenly? If not, you have to continue to remove wood until it works.

BUT: One step at a time — the way you climb a ladder.

After each time you shave along the belly, draw the string a few times and observe the bow. If you are too eager and shave off too much wood at a time, the limb that was too stiff at the first draw will now be too slack and bend too far. Then you have to remove some from the other limb, and the bow will get more and more loose and wobbly and at some point won't hold tension at all.

Also: Always remove just a little wood and immediately check it.

Once I was supposed to build a bow for a good friend, with a draw weight of 35 pounds (15.8-kg). I had selected a difficult piece of elm wood since the bow was supposed to be something special.

After the first processing of the limbs, I proceeded to the tiller. That wasn't all that easy due to the many knotty spots. At one spot I carefully shaved off layer after layer of wood but the profile didn't change. I was still at a 40-pound draw weight. Then I became impatient and removed a whole half-inch at once and even a bit more. When I drew the bow afterwards, I noticed that the limb had become too weak. I then shaved the other one until it worked again, but an ingrown branch had now appeared on that one and the limb became weaker than the first one. I had to process that one again and, before I knew it, I had arrived at a draw weight of less than 30 pounds.

The bow now hangs in a museum where it doesn't matter how it shoots or how strong it is, but rather if it merely looks good.

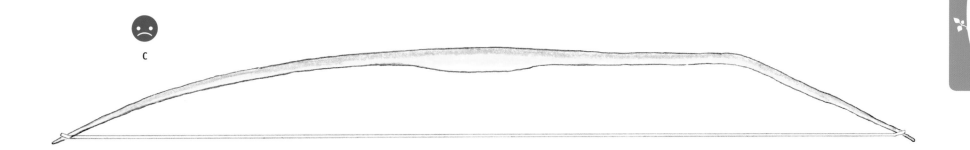

C

If the bow has a weak spot and one of the limbs bends particularly sharp **(C)**, then you have to relieve that spot. Mark the weak area on the front and carefully remove wood in front and behind it until the bend is even again.

When the bow bends uniformly at a twelve-inch draw length (30cm), you should take the time to let it have a day of rest. Unstring the bow for this by placing the bottom end on the ground and bending it slightly so the string is no longer tight. Now you can remove the loop of the bowline knot from the upper end of the bow.

The next day you can continue. Place the bow on the ground with the bottom end, bend it, and hook the loop back onto the limb tip. Now carefully draw the bow further

until you reach 15–16" (40cm). And keep checking the curvature! That also works really well if one person draws the bow and another looks at the curvature from the side. Or you can stand in front of a mirror.

However, you should only draw the bow for very short periods of time and under no circumstance extend it beyond sixteen inches. The proper drawing of a bow isn't all that easy and pulling the bow string up to your ear like Robin Hood in the movie — well, you should not do that until you know how to properly string up your bow. More on this in Chapter 8.

If your bow bends uniformly with a sixteen-inch draw length, let it rest again for a day.

HOLMEGAARD BOW

With the Holmegaard, you proceed similarly; however, you should use even more care and time. And to make the tillering even more precise, you will first build a device to help you with it — the tiller stick.

Procure a piece of roof batten about one yard long. One side should be at least 1-1/2" (4cm) wide. On this side, draw a semicircle on one end (as shown on the sketch at right), so that only two small bridges remain. The handle of your bow should fit into this groove.

Now, drill the first dowel hole twelve inches (30cm) away from the groove, but slanted slightly toward the back. Drill nine additional holes at distances of 1" or 1-1/8" (3cm). Put some glue onto the dowels and place them into the drill holes so that they stick out about 5/8" (1.5cm). Let them dry well — the tiller stick is done.

With it, you can check the curvature of the limbs perfectly without having to hold the bow in your hand.

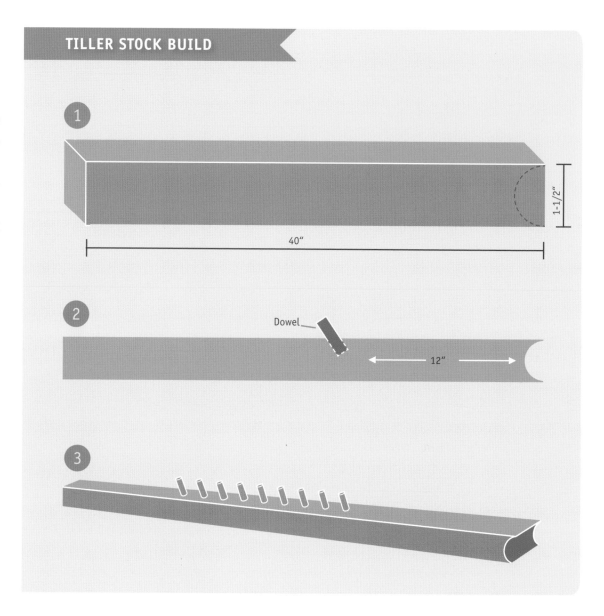

TILLER STOCK BUILD

1

1-1/2"

40"

2

Dowel

12"

3

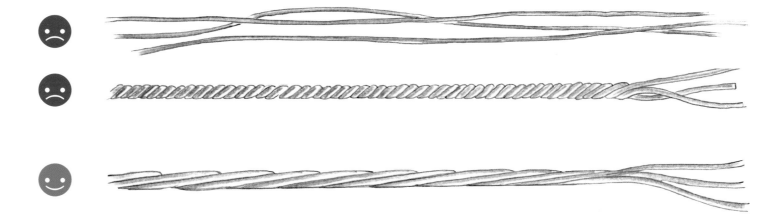

First you have to make a **test or tillering string** for yourself though, as described on page 96. For the Holmegaard, you will need a somewhat stronger string. If you are lucky, you will find thick packaging twine at the home improvement store or supermarket. It should be at least 1/8" (3mm) thick.

Or you can buy a ball of thinner thread and combine the corresponding number of strands; so for a thickness of 1/8", at least three, for a thickness of 1/16" (2mm) two.

Twist the individual strings together loosely, but not too much so they don't fly around. One twist every 12–16" (30-40mm) is enough.

It is also important that the string has a little "give" — that means it shouldn't yield if you pull it apart and it should not stretch. Otherwise, the string will be loose; if you shoot the bow, it will vibrate and hum in your hand. That is annoying. The string should be a good twelve inches (30cm) longer than the bow.

Now, tie a bowline knot at one end as described previously and attach the other end to the lower limb with a clove hitch or timber hitch.

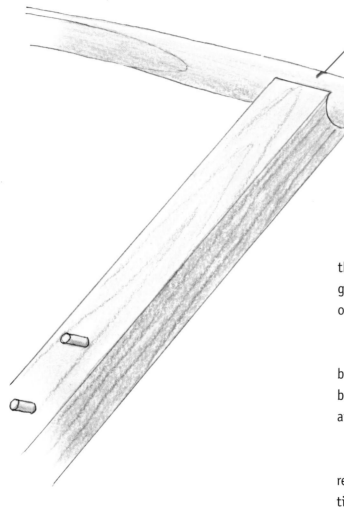

Bow Center

String up the bow so that your hand fits between the handle and the string. Place the bow handle into the groove so that the middle of the bow is lying in the middle of it.

Draw the string to twelve inches (30cm) and place it behind the dowel at the mark for 12". Now you can set the bow, including its tiller stick, onto the ground and look at it from above.

Does your bathroom or kitchen have a floor with rectangular tiles? If so, set the bow onto it so that the tiller stick is parallel to a tile groove. This way you can really see whether the curvature of the bow is correct. If it isn't right yet, work your way toward the ideal curvature as described above.

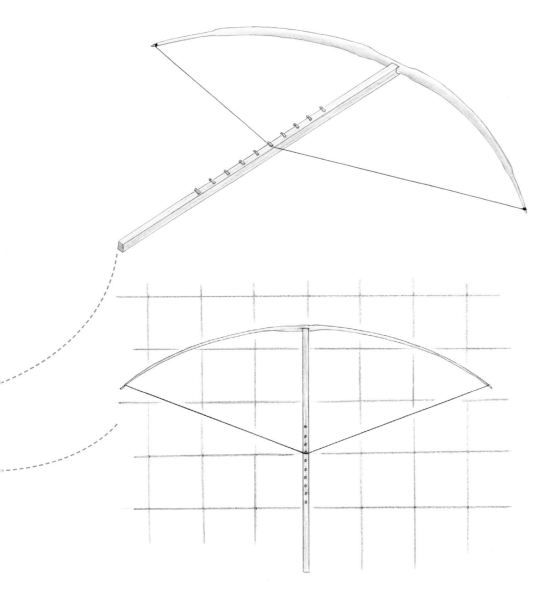

You can use the plane for this. If you discover while drawing the bow that it is still much too powerful, then you have to remove a bit more material at the beginning. Afterward, you should use the scraper. It is ideally suited for removing very thin wood layers very quickly. In contrast to the carving knife or the plane, there is no danger of cutting too far into the wood.

Shaving can also be done with the blade of a knife, but a knife can get dull quickly and you have to always make sure that you don't cut into something you shouldn't with the sharp blade.

If you don't have either a plane or a scraping blade, you can complete this detail work with a grater or file as well. However, there will be a lot of sanding waiting for you afterward, which you can avoid with clean shaving.

Take the bow out of the tiller stick. Clamp the bow into the vise with the handle. Put leather strips or soft wood boards in between, so the handle does not get pressure marks. Remove wood where it is necessary. Then return the bow to the tiller stick and check it. This works fairly well if you orient yourself on the annual rings that can be seen on the sides of the limbs. Try to follow them.

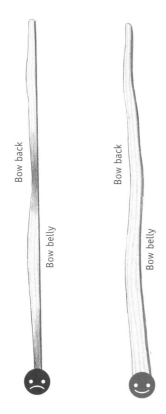

Bow back

Bow belly

Bow back

Bow belly

Where the bow makes a hunched back, you have to remove more wood on the inside; if the bow has a dent on the back, you have to leave more of the material on the belly (see sketch, left).

Under no circumstance may you remove wood from the back of the bow — that is something only for the pros. Also make sure to carefully round all sharp edges on the limbs. Not completely round though, but only on the edge. The expert calls this "breaking the edge" (see sketch, right). In those sharp edges, tensions can build up and that is not good for the bow.

Continue carefully working like this until the bow bends uniformly when drawn to 16" (40cm). You can leave the string on it when shaving if it isn't in the way. Just make sure that you don't accidentally cut it.

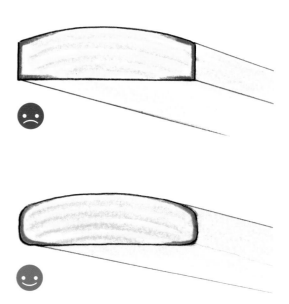

REMEMBER: "Just a quick ..." generally goes wrong! It would have been better to grant yourself the brief moment to clamp the bow into the vise. When working with "sharp objects," you should always "stick with it." Concentrate and work carefully and with forethought.

I have had that happen before. I had finished tillering a very beautiful elm bow and had twisted a matching string. I was already doing the initial shooting when I noticed that one of the limbs was a touch too stiff. Quickly, I took my knife out of my pocket and wanted to remove a hint of wood freehand. I slipped with the knife and the string was almost cut through. Annoying!

I was lucky despite the bad luck: It was "only" the string of the bow, which I had just spent two hours working on. It could have been a sinew in my hand too...

Once you can pull the string up to 16" (40cm) without hurting yourself and the bow bends uniformly, then you should grant it at least one day rest. Unstring it and store it in a cool location that isn't too dry for a few days.

As before, the best spots are under an awning, in the garage, or in an unheated room. The wood has to slowly get used to its new task. You can make a good bow string in the meantime.

Chapter 7

The Bowstring

Here you will find out what you need for a good string and how to attach it to the bow.

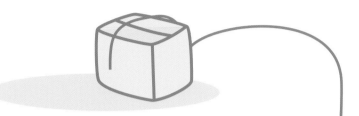

The archers of the past and from foreign continents made their bowstrings out of the most diverse materials.

In the quiver of the iceman "Ötzi," archeologists found a string made of bast fibers. It is 3/16" (4mm) thick and would fit well into the nocks of his arrows. This was probably the string for his unfinished bow. Perhaps he only packed it by accident though, as the bowstrings of the Stone Age consisted of something else. Conceivable would be the fibers of nettles, the flax plant, or they twisted the sinews of animals' intestines or rawhide strips into string. There are even strings made of a split stalk bamboo.

We will make a string out of twine or packaging string. This is affordable and you can get it almost everywhere. It should be made of natural material, not plastic, because plastic is slippery and is hard to knot.

For the Holmegaard, I will also describe a string out of flax yarn.

Important: The string must not have any "give." It must not stretch when you pull on it. When you shoot a string on a bow that has a lot of give then the bow vibrates when you shoot. That is annoying and leads to imprecise shooting.

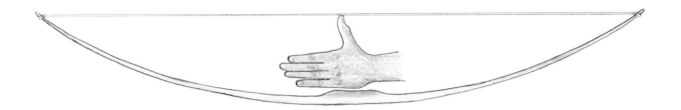

THE BENT STICK

For a very simple bow, a simple string is good enough. Tie the string as described to the bow, but this time string it so that your hand fits between the handle and the string with your thumb extended thumb (see sketch above).

Make the loop of the bowline knot just wide enough for it to fit over the upper limb. Then you can leave the string on the bow later on. Tighten the clove hitch on the lower limb and secure it with one or two half hitches as shown on the sketch.

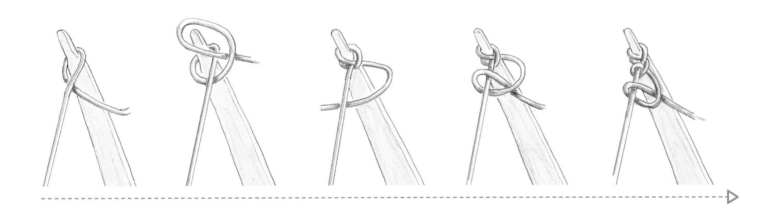

HOLMEGAARD BOW

For the Holmegaard, you need a more stable string since it will be stronger than the "simple bow."

For a simple string, you can use packaging twine. It should be at least 1/8" (3mm) thick. You can also make it out of several thin strings. For this, twist the individual strands together into one. Make a bowline knot at one end, the loop of which fits over the upper limb, and then tie the string as described above to the lower limb of the bow with a clove hitch.

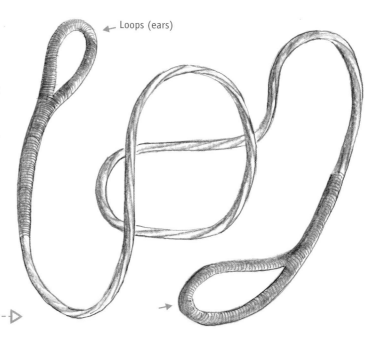

Loops (ears)

A SPLICED STRING

One option to attach the string to the bow without a knot is the use of a string with two loops (or ears) at the end. The loops are spliced, which means the end of the string is shaped into a loop and the loose end of the string is threaded in.

Such a string is not exactly easy to make, but once you have done it a few times, it isn't that difficult anymore. Many archers make the loops with the so-called Flemish splice. I splice the loops a bit differently, similar to how a sailor splices a loop into a rope.

For such a string, you will need thin thread, about 1/16" (1mm) thick. Flax yarn is very well suited and is used for sewing hiking boots. You can find it on the Internet if you search for "special double twisting raw gray" or at a leather shop in your area. Mostly, it is available as 20/8 or 18/3 yarn.

It is said that the string should be able to withstand at least four times the draw weight of the bow. For a bow with a draw weight of about twenty pounds, you will need to make a string out of four individual 20/8 yarns.

And that is done as follows:

String the test string onto the bow in a way that your hand fits between the handle and the string with extended thumb (see illustration on page 111).

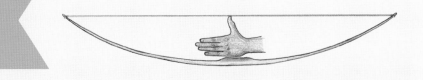

Chord length.

Measure the length of the string from the center of the loop to the other center of the loop with a yardstick. That is the length of your string.

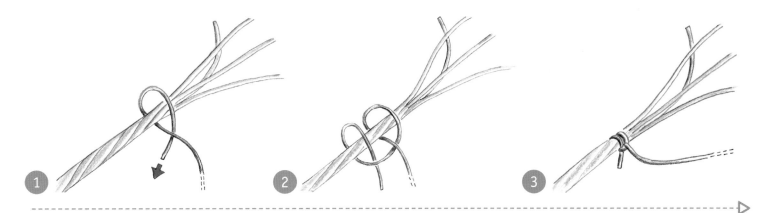

1. Cut four strands off the thread or the flax yarn according to the measurement of the length of the string plus 12" (30cm). Cut off an approximately 59-inch-long (1.5m) piece of thin ply yarn.

2. Five inches (12cm) from the end of the strands tie a clove hitch with the ply yarn around the four strands.

3. Pull the knot so tight that they are bundled and cannot slip.

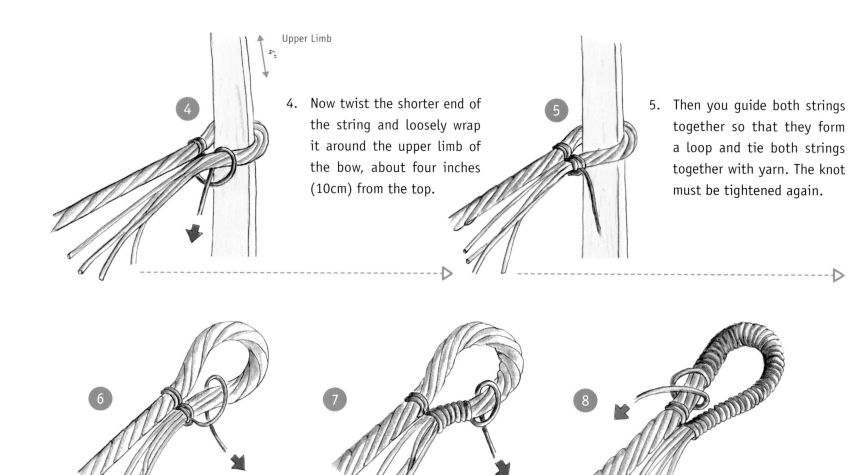

Upper Limb

4"

4. Now twist the shorter end of the string and loosely wrap it around the upper limb of the bow, about four inches (10cm) from the top.

5. Then you guide both strings together so that they form a loop and tie both strings together with yarn. The knot must be tightened again.

6–8. Now take the loose end of the thin ply yarn and wind the entire loop with it. This wrap prevents the loop from rubbing through and the string from tearing. You have to pull the string tight after each wrap.

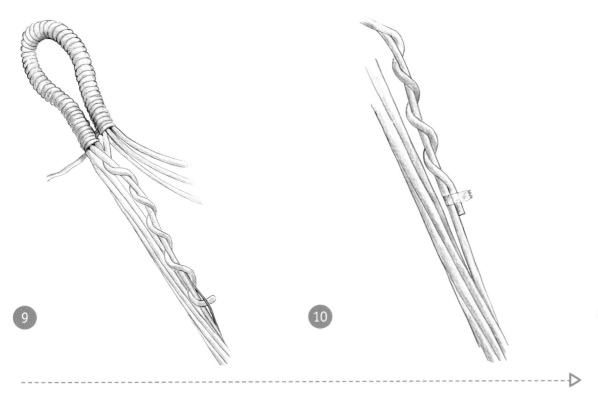

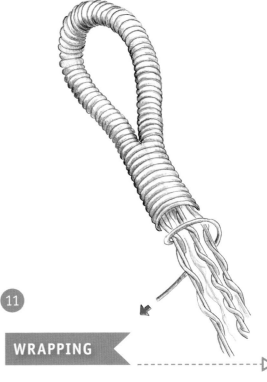

WRAPPING

9. Once the loop has been wound, hang it over a nail/wooden stick. Then take a strand from the shorter end and wind it around one of the strands of the longer end in a spiral pattern.

    To keep the wrapping from unraveling, pull the end of the strand through the wrapped strand as in the sketch.

10. If you don't use yarn or the strand cannot be opened to pull the loose strand through, you can also glue it with a tiny piece of tape to the other strand.

    The strands should be twisted together over a length of about 3" (8cm). Let the ends of the strands show at the end of the string.

11. Once you have wound all four of the loose strands in this manner around the four fixed ones and have fastened them, wrap the entire splice with thin ply yarn. Sailors call this **tackling**. Make sure that the wrap turns out tight and that the individual loops of the wrap lie tight against each other. That doesn't just look good, but also ensures that the splice holds.

12: **Wrap the final half-inch of the yarn wrap as follows:** While wrapping, place a pencil along the string and wrap it in with it. Don't wrap it too tightly or you won't be able to remove the pencil.

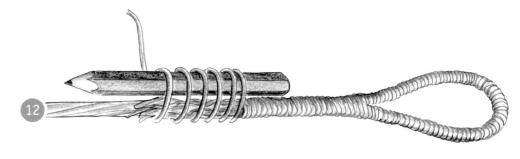

13: After wrapping 1/2", carefully pull out the pencil and thread the loose end of the yarn through the wrap so that it is seen about 4" (10cm) on the other side.

14: Now tighten the loose wrap row by row.

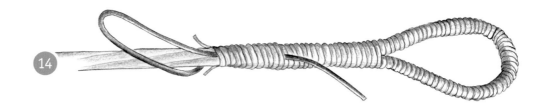

15: When everything is tight, pull on the loose end of the yarn until everything has disappeared under the wrap. Cut off the rest of the yarn and the individual string strands that are hanging out. This way you have a beautiful wrap that is attached invisibly and holds well.

Cut off rest of yarn that's hanging out.

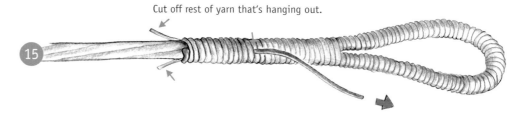

One of the loops is now finished. Hang it over a nail or wooden stick and tighten the loose strands. Mark the string length plus 1/2" (1cm) on the yarn, measured from the inner edge of the finished loop.

Twist the four strands lightly with each other (see illustration on page 103), so they create a string.

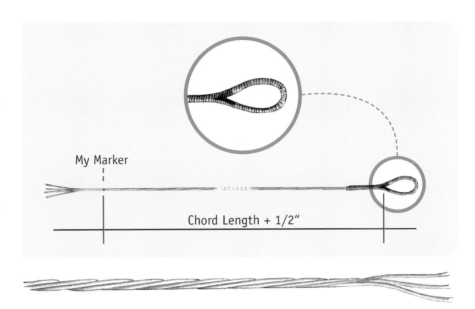

My Marker

Chord Length + 1/2"

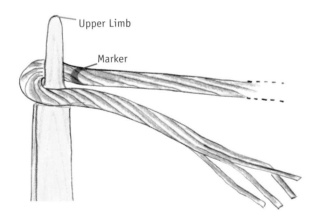

Upper Limb

Marker

Again, cut a piece of yarn about 47 inches long (1.2m). Hold the length mark on the string onto the lower limb and shape a loop with the loose end. It should be large enough to loosely fit onto the limb. Knot both strings to the yarn with a clove hitch, splice the individual strands, and then wrap the second loop like the first one. Now your string is finished.

The large loop goes on the upper limb and is merely pushed toward the top for stringing the bow. The small loop goes on the lower limb and remains there.

Chapter 8

Stringing the Bow and Precise Tiller

Learn how to string the bow, hold it properly, and finish tillering it.

Up to now we have always set the bow onto the ground with the lower limb to string it. However, that is not that good for the bow.

I keep seeing bad movies in which disheveled Stone Age people use their bows as hiking sticks. Or they throw the bow with the quiver carelessly into the corner of the cave when they get home.

What would happen if you pushed the limb like a hiking stick repeatedly into the rocky or moist ground?

Exactly: The tip would get soft or get worn off rather quickly. The bow would keep getting shorter until the string no longer fits.

So: complete nonsense. You carry a bow in your hand while hiking and make sure that it doesn't bang against anything. The slightest damage could lead to the bow breaking and then you could no longer hunt, and without hunting there is less to eat!

THAT IS WHY YOU STRING THE BOW LIKE THIS (FOR RIGHT-HANDED PEOPLE):

1: You pushed the finished string over the upper limb with the large loop and placed the small loop on the lower limb top. Now hold the bow at a slight angle in front of you so that the string is facing up. Step into the bow with the left leg.

2: Put the lower limb tip on the front of the arch of your right foot so that the limb rests on your right shin and is not sitting on the ground!

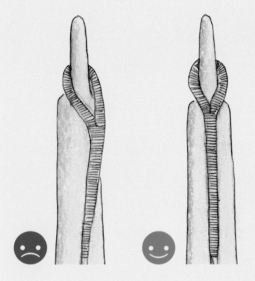

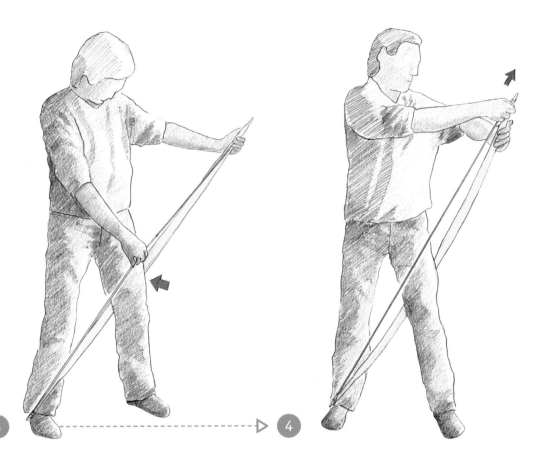

3   **3:** Then place the handle of the bow into the left back of the knee, but...**only the handle and precisely into the back of the knee**. Pay attention to this!

4   **4:** Now you can comfortably bend the bow toward you and push the loop of the string up the limb until it sits on the tip.

Check again whether the loops are sitting properly on the tips, so that the string rests centered on the limb.

Left-handed people do everything the other way around.

Check again whether the bow is strung properly. Can you fit your hand with the thumb extended between the bow and the string?

If the hand doesn't fit between them, the string got too short and you will have to make a new one that fits. It will probably be too long though since we added a half-inch (1cm). You can shorten the string again by twisting it more.

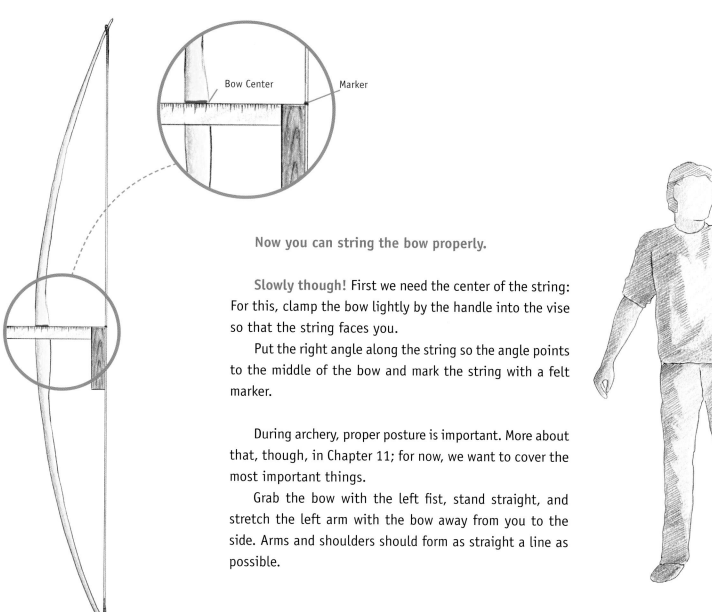

Bow Center Marker

Now you can string the bow properly.

Slowly though! First we need the center of the string: For this, clamp the bow lightly by the handle into the vise so that the string faces you.

Put the right angle along the string so the angle points to the middle of the bow and mark the string with a felt marker.

During archery, proper posture is important. More about that, though, in Chapter 11; for now, we want to cover the most important things.

Grab the bow with the left fist, stand straight, and stretch the left arm with the bow away from you to the side. Arms and shoulders should form as straight a line as possible.

Grab the string with the right hand. There are several ways of holding the string; I prefer the so-called **Mediterranean loose:**

Three fingers hold the string, and the pointer finger sits above the arrow (in this case above the marked point on the string). The middle and ring fingers sit below that; the thumb is not used. Only the fingertips are holding the string.

Now you can draw the bow...very softly at first, and then a bit more.

The bow has to get used to working. If you were chased out of bed at lightning speed in the morning and immediately sent to school without breakfast, then you probably would have trouble too. Therefore, you should carefully warm up the bow, so draw it halfway a few times (but don't let the string snap back, see page 49) and only then draw the string to the tip of your nose.

How is the bow? Can it be drawn comfortably?

If you notice that you can't draw it all the way (at least to the tip of your nose) or you can't draw it without trembling, then it is too strong for you. It is not bending enough yet. You need to tiller it a bit more until it works. Always watch the evenness of the curvature, and never remove too much wood at once...keep checking, checking, and checking again.

When you have tillered your bow to the point where it can be drawn comfortably and the limbs bend evenly, unstring the bow.

The procedure is the same — left leg into the bow, lower limb against the right shin, handle into the left back of the knee, bend the bow, and slide the upper loop down the limb. This time we want to take off the string though, so bend the bow and remove the upper loop from the limb tip. Also remove the lower loop.

Make sure the twisted string doesn't untwist. You can hang it up on a stick by the loops.

Now you can sand the bow.

First with the 80 grit paper, sand until all the rough spots are smooth. Then you give the bow a final polish with the 160 grit (150 grit works too), until the bow is nice and smooth everywhere. Especially the edges have to be nicely rounded.

Now you can seal the bow so the surface is protected and the bow can get wet on occasion. Milking grease works really well here. It isn't sticky, doesn't get rancid, and protects very well. You can purchase milking grease at a farming supply store. If you can't get any, you can also use cooking oil.

Put some milking grease (or oil) onto a rag and rub the entire bow with it thoroughly, several times if desired. If you rub harder with the rag, you create frictional heat. That is good because then the grease will penetrate the wood better.

By the way, you should rub the bow at least every half year with milking grease or oil. It loves that!

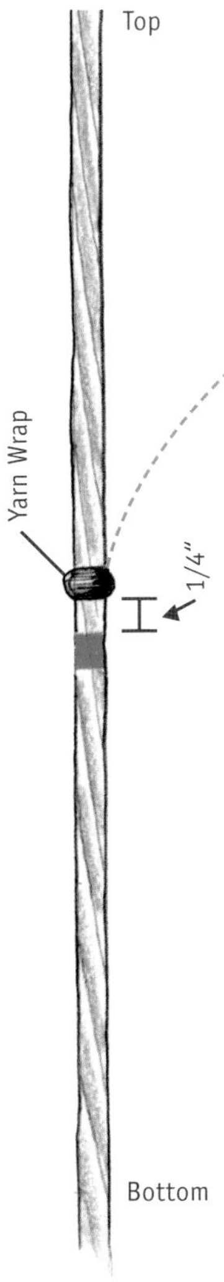

Top

Yarn Wrap

1/4"

Bottom

Place a small yarn wrap on the string 1/4" (5mm) above the center mark and secure it with two half hitches and a bit of glue. That is the so-called nocking point. The arrow is later placed precisely below the nocking point onto the string.

Wrap the string in the area 1-1/4" (3cm) above and approximately 2-1/2" (6cm) below the nock point with yarn (right). Over the course of time, this will prevent the string from being worn through where the arrow rests.

The string can also use some protection. Rub it with beeswax and rub it hard a few times with the rag. The frictional heat lets the wax penetrate the string well. Rub it again with milking grease.

Now you should let the bow rest a few more days and use the time to build really good arrows.

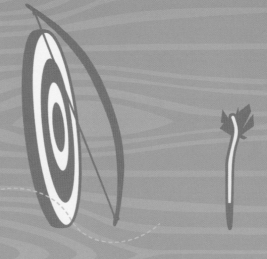

Chapter 9

The Arrows

Learn why a bad bow with good arrows shoots better than a good bow with bad arrows. Also learn what materials you need for a good arrow and how to make one.

There are quite a few men who brag about their muscle strength and think they are the greatest when they have big muscles all over.

When one of those braggarts took up the pose in the past, we always pointed at the arm muscles and said:

"What good are the 10,000 volt here, if over here" — and we pointed at the head then — "there is no lamp!"

It is similar with the bow and arrow. What good is the best and strongest bow if you shoot bad arrows?

The bow "merely" stores energy and releases it again. The arrow, however, is supposed to reach the target, and it can only

do that if it flies well. And it only flies well if it is made well. So it is easier to shoot a good arrow with a bad bow than the other way around.

A good bow with mismatched arrows — that is like running 1,000 yards with bare feet or listening to music through the telephone speaker.

DRAW LENGTH

First you have to find out how long the arrow should be. Determine your draw length — the distance that you can draw your bow — as follows:

• Take an arrow shaft (pine dowel or shoot) and place it vertically along your breastbone (the indentation in the front on your chest), with the thick end of the shoot.

• Stand upright, stretch your arms horizontally away from your body, and hold the shaft in between. Where your middle fingers touch the arrow shaft, **mark the shaft**. That is your draw length. Add 1" (2cm) more and saw the shaft off at the mark.

Marker

For the
Bent Stick

For a good arrow you need:

- -

✓ **Pine Dowel** Ø = 1/4–5/16"
(6-8mm), 40" (1m) long

✓ **Yardstick, pencil**

✓ **Hacksaw**

✓ 2 whole **Feathers**

✓ **Thin yarn**

✓ **Glue**

✓ **Sharp knife**

✓ Poss. **Iron nail**, 3/16" thick

✓ **Multi-purpose pliers**

A pine dowel, 1/4" or 5/16" (6 or 8mm), is available at any home improvement store. You can get by with a 1/4" diameter; if that isn't not available, you can use 5/16" too. However, you have to select them carefully.

You should pay attention to the following:

✓ The sticks have to be straight

✓ They must not include any branch knots or large twirls

✓ The wood grain must run from one end to the other

If that is not the case, the stick was cut out of the wood so that the annual rings were cut off at an angle. This means it will break soon; the same with branch knots, so take your time when selecting. Look at one hundred sticks and choose the ten most beautiful ones before you take the first ones.

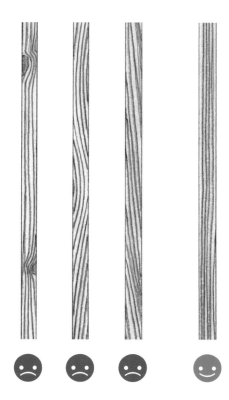

Have you checked all the shafts and sawed them off to length? Good. Now you will make the nock on an arrow, the string notch.

1 For this you look at an end face:

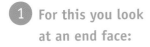

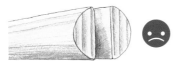

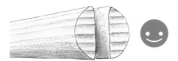

What direction are the annual rings running in? You will have to know this because the string notch is supposed to be at a right angle to it. This prevents the arrow from splitting when the string puts pressure on the notch, and is very important.

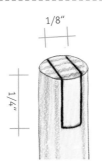

1/8"

1/4"

2 Draw a slot with a thickness of about 1/8" (3mm) onto the cross-cut wood, which should be about 1/4" (6mm) long on the side.

3 Hold the arrow tightly, on a table edge or a tree trunk would be best, and saw a notch with a hacksaw. Watch your fingers!

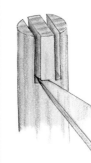

4 Stab the knife carefully into the side between the saw cuts.

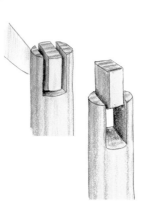

5 Then at some time you can break away the wooden block. **Caution:** Do not stab into the sides of the string notch, otherwise they will break off later.

6 Fold the sand paper once and sand the string notch until it is smooth, especially the notch bottom. Make sure that the edges of the notch become nicely rounded, so the string doesn't have to bend too sharply around the corner. You can sharpen the other end of the arrow, but not too sharp, or the tip will break off immediately.

Find feathers while walking through the forest, along the lake or the ocean, on fields (here likely under power poles, as the birds like to sit there because of the view), on a farm that keeps geese or turkeys, or in Grandpa's chicken coop.

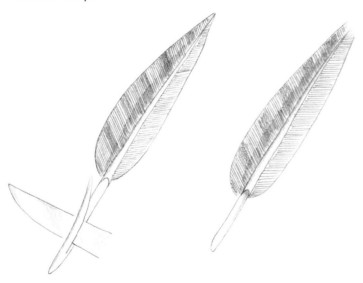

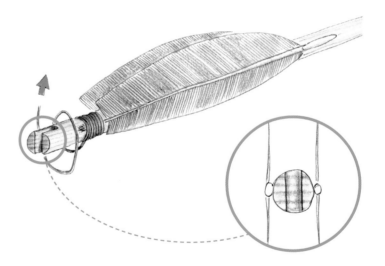

The feathers should be at least 4" long (10cm). Take two equally long feathers and carve the quill away on one side halfway.

Tie them with the thin yarn on both sides to the back of the arrow where the nock is. The feather quill points toward the tip; the feathers are parallel to the string notch.

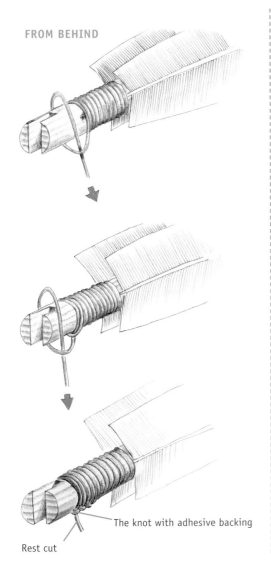

The knot with adhesive backing

Rest cut

Keep a distance of at least 3/4" (2cm) from the nock, so that the feathers aren't in the way when you grab the arrow.

Wrap one of the ends of the yarn in with it (see below) and tie a double clove hitch (or four half hitches) at the end of the wrap around the shaft.

The wrap should end under the string notch, so you can keep the string notch from splitting.

Secure the knots with some glue. Attach the feathers in the same manner at the front.

Make sure that the wrap completely covers the feather quills. Otherwise the sharp edges of the feather quills will cut your hand when shooting!

IN FRONT

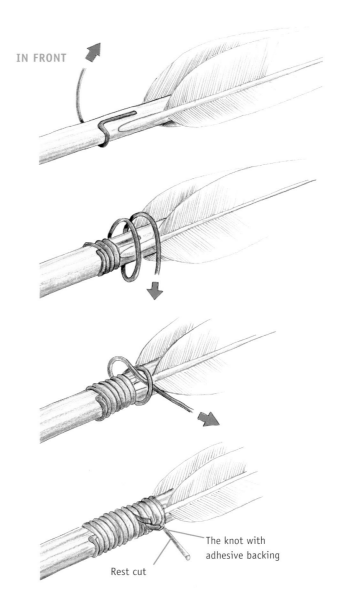

The knot with adhesive backing

Rest cut

Holmegaard

For a good arrow you will need:

- -

- ✓ **Sprout from a hazel bush**, a **guelder rose**, or other bushes
- ✓ **Yardstick**, **pencil**
- ✓ **Rose scissors** or a small **garden saw**
- ✓ **Wooden board**
- ✓ **Hacksaw** or other detail saw
- ✓ 3 whole **feathers**
- ✓ **Contact glue** (e.g., Pattex®)
- ✓ **Linen yarn**
- ✓ Sharp **knife**
- ✓ **Sandpaper** 80 grit
- ✓ **Scissors**
- ✓ Small piece of **hard cardboard**, a **triangle**, **compass**
- ✓ **Felt marker** (e.g., Sharpie®) in various colors
- ✓ **Milking grease**
- ✓ Poss. **bone** or **antler piece**
- ✓ **File**
- ✓ Waterproof **wood glue** or **glue**

For the Holmegaard, we want to make arrows out of the sprouts of bushes.

Of course, you can also construct very simple arrows out of pine sticks, perhaps with triple fletching (see page 148). I prefer natural arrows though. They fit the bow better and are harder to produce, just like the Holmegaard, so a challenge for your craft skills. They also look much prettier.

You can find suitable sprouts, or young shoots, that grow in the middle of bushes in parks, hedges, your garden, your neighbor's garden, at the edges of forests, and in street embankments. As with the working piece for the bow you should ask for permission before cutting it and, of course, respect growth seasons and nature preserves.

Usually, you can cut one or two arrow shafts out of a bush without anyone getting upset.

For arrow shafts, the following wood varieties work best:

Dogwood
(cornus sanguinea)

Good arrow wood, dogwood grows almost anywhere.

Wayfaring Tree
(viburnum lantana)

Very good arrow wood, grows on chalky soils, so it isn't available everywhere. Ötzi's arrows were made of this.

Guelder Rose
(viburnum opulus)

More widespread than the wayfaring tree, but it's not as well suited and is quite light.

Hazel
(corylus avellana)

Hazel bushes are at every corner; the wood is quite good, but tends to get brittle with age.

The best time to harvest shafts is wintertime as with the wood for the bow, particularly the time around the first new moon in a year.

Since there are no leaves on the bushes then, you can recognize more easily whether there are usable sprouts growing in a bush, and there is less juice in the wood.

Take your time during the selection process and pay attention to the following:

✓ The sprouts should be as straight as possible
✓ They should be about 3/8–1/2" (9-10mm) thick
✓ They should not have any branch starts, single leaves are no problem (see near right)
They must not display any growth damage such as circumvallation or abrasion spots (see center right)
✓ They should have a uniform increase in thickness: A shoot is by nature always a bit thinner at the upper end than at the bottom
✓ Only select those that are as evenly thick as possible over a length of at least 20" (50cm). They must have a diameter of at least 3/8" (9mm) at the thin end though

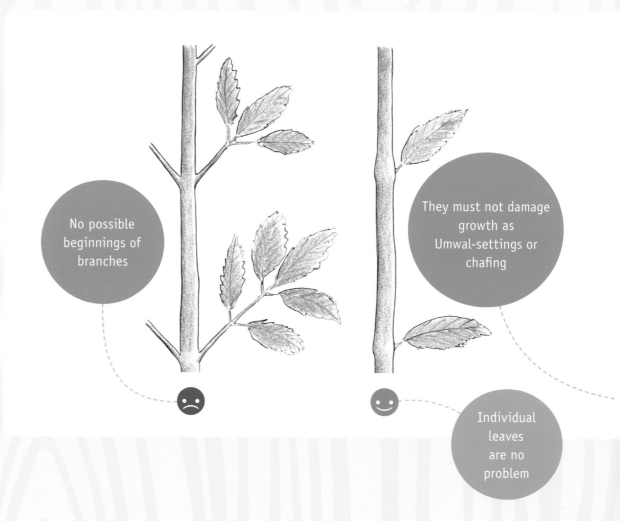

No possible beginnings of branches

They must not damage growth as Umwal-settings or chafing

Individual leaves are no problem

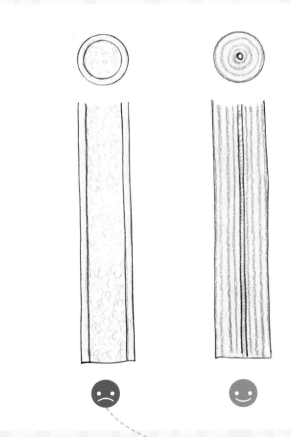

When you have found an appropriate **sprout**, cut it with a garden saw or rose cutters.

Shorten it (measuring from the thicker end) to about 40" (1m) and seal the cut surfaces, such as the working piece for the bow, with glue or paint. Then place it in a dry cool location, where it is exposed to the wind but not the sun, and let it dry for a few days.

Those that have a barky outer layer over this length and are still very green on top and are full of fresh leaves should be left standing.

With those, the pith is still very thick at the upper end, so it does not have a stable layer in the notch yet.

Let the shoots dry for about three to four weeks in the bark. During this time you can occasionally straighten them out again. Almost no sprout is completely straight by nature. You can correct minor bends by bending the arrow slightly in the opposite direction until it remains straight. Severe bends or sharp kinks are hard to fix — you shouldn't take along such shafts to begin with.

Bend the shafts until they remain straight. **But be careful:** In particular, with the wayfaring tree, the shaft bends a little between branch knots.

You can ignore that if the shaft overall is straight along the entire length. It is very difficult to straighten these slight bends, often the shaft breaks while doing it.

After four weeks of drying and straightening, you can scrape the bark off the shafts with a pocket knife, but be careful not to cut into the wood.

Once the bark is off, you can straighten the shafts for a few more days until they are finally dry. Those that aren't straight by now won't ever be straight.

Watch out: If the bark is still on the shaft and you hear a crack during straightening, that is normal because the bark shrinks during drying. You should still check the shaft afterward, though.

However, if a peeled shaft cracks during straightening, you have bent it too far. It tore. It probably is no longer usable, so put it aside. Only flawless shafts receive the opportunity to become good and reliable arrows.

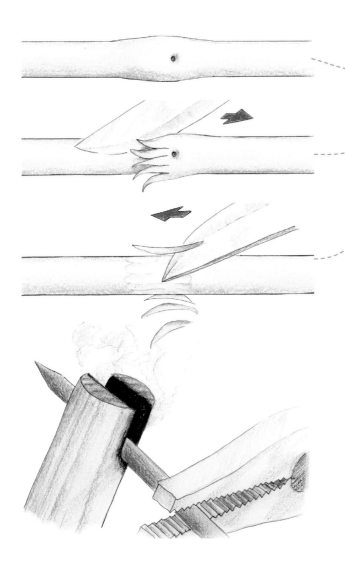

When the shafts have dried nicely, you can carve off the branch knots. Carve off the bulges with a sharp knife, but only remove wafer thin shavings and only carve up to the center of the branch.

Flip the arrow over and carve the bulges off from the other side, again only up to the center of the branch. This way you prevent yourself from cutting beyond the branch and into the wood. Once the shaft is carved smooth, sand it completely with the 80 grit sand paper all the way around.

One last check: Look the shaft over again from all sides, bend it a little, and check whether it can handle it. The arrow has to be flexible because of the bow paradox (see Chapter 2). If it cannot be bent at all, it is too stiff. It would fly really poorly. If it maintains the bend, then it is too soft and is also useless. After a few shots with different arrows and different spine values, you will get a feel for which shaft works and which one does not. It must not have any tears or weak spots.

Everything okay? Then you can attach the **string notch** at the thinner end now, as described on page 131.

An alternative is to **burn the notch** into the nock. For this, heat an iron nail with a 3/16" (4mm) diameter by the campfire. Grasp it with multi-purpose pliers and hold it against the end of the shaft until an approximately 1/4" (6mm) deep notch is burnt in (see sketch bottom left). You may have to reheat the nail several times.

Caution: Danger of injury — and watch out for the fire!

A BONE HEAD

You can simply sharpen the thicker end of the shaft. Or you can carefully drill a hole into the pith and stick a nail into it so that the head of the nail sticks out in front (see sketch at left) — not the tip of the nail! That would be a dangerous weapon, but more on that in Chapter 11.

It is a bit more effort to insert a tip and that is done this way: Get a straight bone from a young animal, such as the middle foot bone or a shin from the slaughterhouse/butcher/meat cutter.

Ask the butcher to saw a straight splinter out of it for you that is about 3/16" thick, 1/4" long, and about 3/4" wide.

At home, place it into boiling water for about one minute; let it cool down and then dry in an airy shady place for a day. Next, you turn it into this shape, using a rasp, file, and sandpaper (see sketch on right).

The tip is supposed to be as wide as the arrow shaft is thick in the front and at least half as thick. Don't make it too pointed because it may break off easily. At the end that is later inserted into the arrow shaft, leave the surface rough so the glue will hold better.

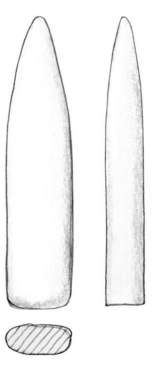

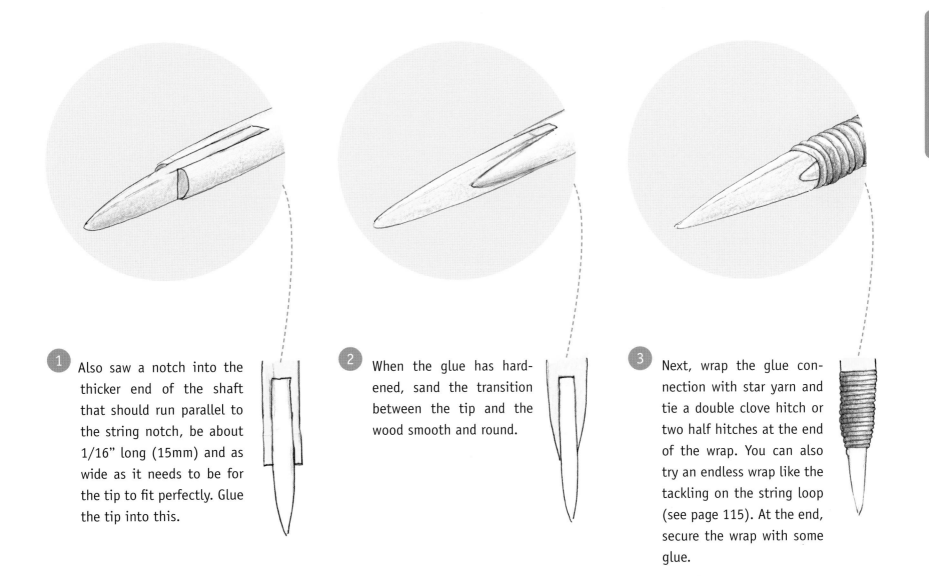

1 Also saw a notch into the thicker end of the shaft that should run parallel to the string notch, be about 1/16" long (15mm) and as wide as it needs to be for the tip to fit perfectly. Glue the tip into this.

2 When the glue has hardened, sand the transition between the tip and the wood smooth and round.

3 Next, wrap the glue connection with star yarn and tie a double clove hitch or two half hitches at the end of the wrap. You can also try an endless wrap like the tackling on the string loop (see page 115). At the end, secure the wrap with some glue.

Now for the hardest part — the fletching. Of course, you can also attach a "lazy man's" fletching to your arrow as described previously for the simple arrow. However, arrows have been made for thousands of years with radially attached feathers because they fly better.

There are some with just two guide feathers, but also with four and more. Those arrows are called "Fluflu" and they were used for hunting birds (see sketch above).

Due to the many feather vanes at the back, their air resistance is very high. They are soon slowed down, so they don't fly as far and can be easily found again. If you don't want to shoot up high into the air, but rather quickly and far, then the feathers should be as small as they need to be to prevent unnecessary breaking but large enough for control. For that is the real task of the feathers — to control the flight of the arrow.

Perhaps you once — as we used to — threw reeds through the air like spears. For us, the ones that still had their tuft on top, always flew the best. When the reed flies through the air, it has greater resistance in the back than in the front due to the tuft at the end. This keeps the reed on a flight path and from going into a tailspin. Many flying objects use this principle. They have a control unit at the rear.

In physics, it is also true that an object is better at flying straight if it rotates around its own longitudinal axis. (This is only true for flying objects without airfoils or wings, otherwise passenger airplanes would have to rotate too and passengers would suffer from motion sickness.)

For a gun, grooves in the gun barrel ensure that the bullet rotates during flight. With an arrow, the feathers accomplish this since they are attached to the shaft at an angle. During flight, the air pours over them from the side, which rotates the arrow.

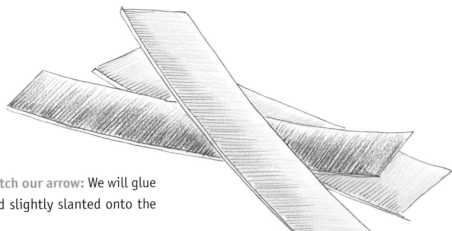

And this is how we will fletch our arrow: We will glue three feather vanes radially and slightly slanted onto the tail of our shaft.

Not all feathers are suited to radial fletching. They have to be reasonably stable, and that eliminates quite a few birds as providers. Most of the feathers you find while going for a walk outside are not usable. Pigeons, chickens, ducks, and even crows and buzzards have feathers that are too soft. They would break, not control.

Suitable are: Swan, goose, turkey.

Swans and wild geese live on many ponds, lakes, and rivers. Their feathers can easily be found outdoors in nature when the birds are changing their plumage during the so-called molting. That occurs during late spring. So if you walk along the shore or beach during the summer, you have a good chance of collecting feathers for a few arrows.

Turkeys and domestic geese are often slaughtered in the fall, so it is worth asking a farmer or your neighbor then about getting some of their feathers. If you can, freeze the feathers in a freezer bag for a week; then mites and moths have no chance of destroying them.

Those who don't have any of these options can order feathers — look on the Internet for merchants. You need feathers that are full length; three for each arrow, two of them in one color and one in another. So for ten arrows, you would need twenty white and ten red feathers (more about that later). Buy a few extra as reserve in case something goes wrong.

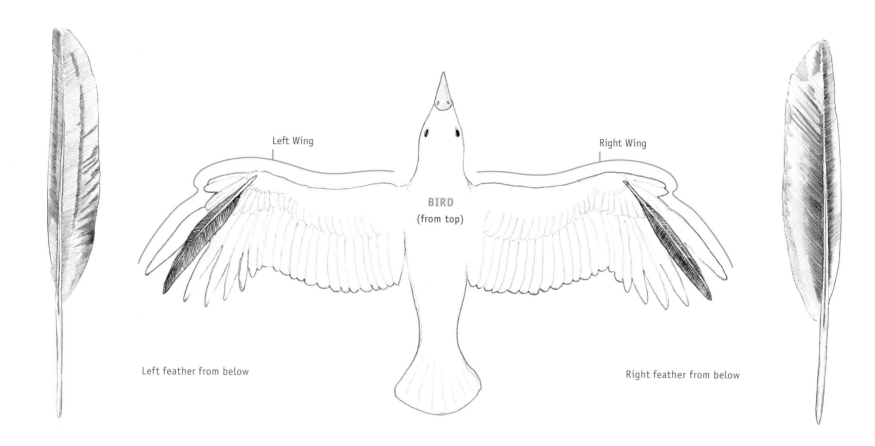

Left Wing

Right Wing

BIRD
(from top)

Left feather from below

Right feather from below

Important: The feathers must all stem from one wing! Left feathers are bent opposite of right ones, as illustrated above.

In order to effect a rotation around the arrow's own axis due to the slant, they of course have to have the same slant. If they were bent differently, they would brake.

Also: For an arrow, or better yet an entire batch of arrows, use only feathers from the same wing. Whether left or right, doesn't matter. While they say that left-handed archers should only use left feathers and right-handed archers only right ones, that belongs into the pro-archer department. Let's be happy if we can organize a few nice matching feathers.

FLAGS MANUFACTURE

If you use natural feathers, you have to make the vanes now. This is how it is done: Draw a straight line onto the wooden board and mark a length of 3" (8cm) on it.

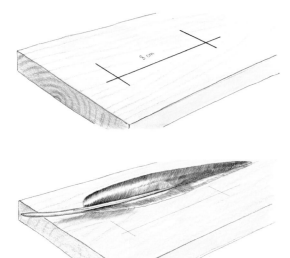

Place the feather onto the wooden board, with the hollow concavity upward.

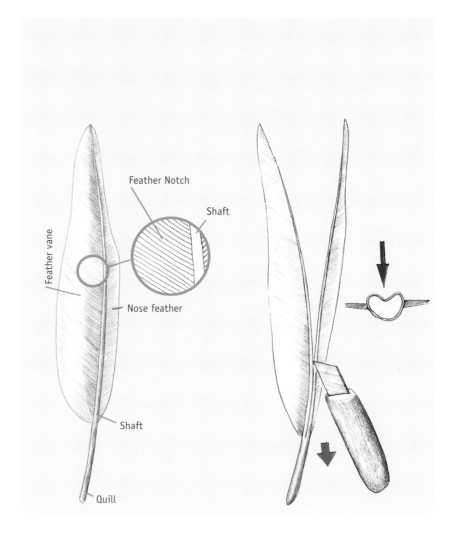

The shaft has a notch on this side in almost all feathers. Cut the shaft open lengthwise along this notch — always stay in the middle. For this you can even use a carpet knife, but only for this! Carpet knives and craft knives are not meant for wood carving.

You start at the back end of the feather and work toward the quill. You don't need the narrow feather vane, the so-called nose feather, but rather the other wide one.

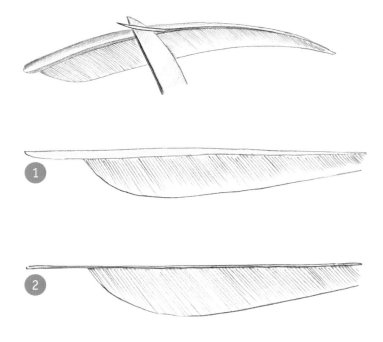

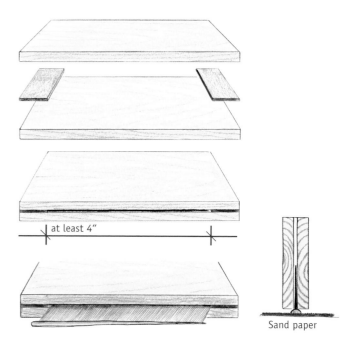

at least 4"

Sand paper

Now you have to cut the shaft as narrow as possible so that there is practically only a ribbon left, which holds the individual barbs (branches) of the vane.

For this, carve off, coil, and shaft carefully on the side — always away from you, never toward you! Make sure that the knife doesn't cut too deeply into the shaft. Scrape the white substance in the interior of the shaft that looks like Styrofoam® smooth with the knife.

At the end, sand the shaft smooth. You can also sand the shaft thin without carving. Take two thin, narrow boards and glue a piece of cardboard in between on both sides and attach them with tape (as shown on the sketch).

Place the feather with the vane in the slot between the boards and sand half the shaft thin on one piece of sand paper, but not so thin though that the "band" becomes sloppy.

Once the band is narrow and sufficiently thin, put the vane onto the mark on the wooden board and cut it off at the markings.

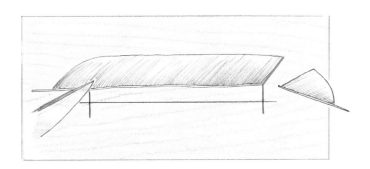

At the front end of the shaft, take the barbs a length of 3/8" (1cm) between your thumb and the pointer finger and tear off the rib against the slant.

3/8"

At the back end, carefully cut off the barbs from the rib at a length of 3/8" (1cm).

3/8"

Finally, cut the vane into the shape in the sketch. Now your vane is prepared for fletching.

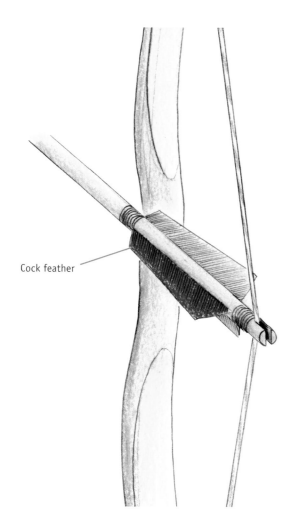

Cock feather

As previously mentioned, for every arrow, you need three of them: one of those should be in another color so you will always recognize it. That will be the so-called **cock feather** (left). It stands vertical to the string notch and always points away from the bow when the arrow is placed on the bow.

This serves to prevent any feather from having to slide directly along the bow when the arrow is shot. The cock feather isn't diverted as much since the other two feathers now lay at a slant to the bow string above and below it (right).

If you have dark (grey goose) and light (swan) feathers, then good. If you only have white ones, you can dye one of them. A felt marker works pretty well. It should be waterproof. You can also dip feathers into fabric dye or even in berry juice. Blueberries, elderberries, and black currants make a very good coloring paste.

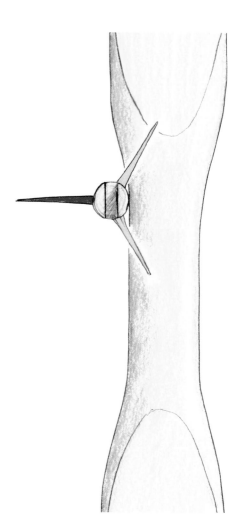

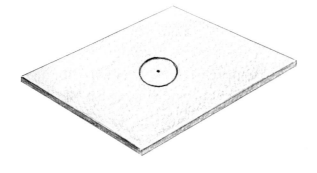

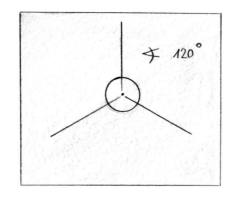

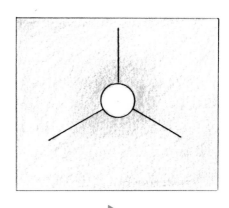

1 Now the feathers are attached to the arrow shaft. First you need a small piece of stiff cardboard. Draw a dot into the center and make a circle around it with the compass. The circle diameter should be 3/8" (9-10mm), definitely a bit larger than the diameter of the shaft.

2 Divide the circle with the triangle into three equal pie pieces at an angle of 120°. Draw the separation lines past the edge of the circle.

3 Now cut out the circle in the middle.

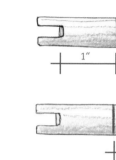

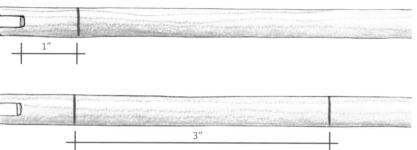

Now make a pencil mark about one inch (2cm) in front of the string notch and draw a circle around the shaft.

Measure three inches (8cm) from there toward the front and draw a line all the way around the shaft here as well.

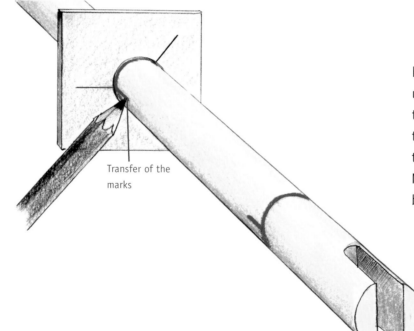

Transfer of the marks

Stick the template onto the shaft and hold it onto the front line. Turn the template until one of the three lines is perpendicular to the string notch. Hold on to the arrow and the template and transfer the three lines onto the shaft. Do the same thing at the back end. Now connect the three front and the three back marks.

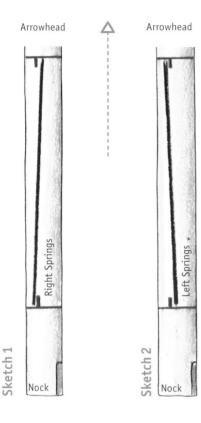

Sketch 1

Arrowhead

Right Springs

Nock

Sketch 2

Arrowhead

Left Springs

Nock

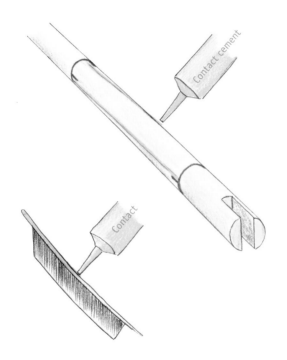

Contact cement

Contact

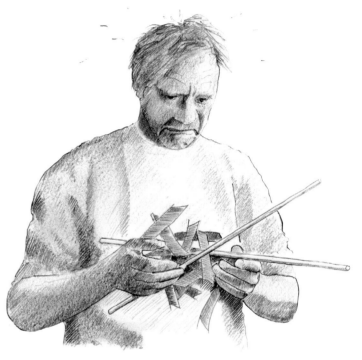

If you use right feathers, draw along the shaft past the markings as shown in **Sketch 1**; if you use left feathers, follow **Sketch 2**. Now the three lines should be visible on the shaft, slanted and at an equal distance to each other.

Glue the feathers on with a contact cement. For this, put a thin layer of glue onto the pencil marks on the shaft and brush the band of the three-feather vanes with glue.

You have to work very cleanly there. Be careful that the contact cement really only gets onto the lines on the arrow and feather shafts, not on your hands. Otherwise, everything will stick together in a large lump afterward. Let the glue dry the prescribed amount of time.

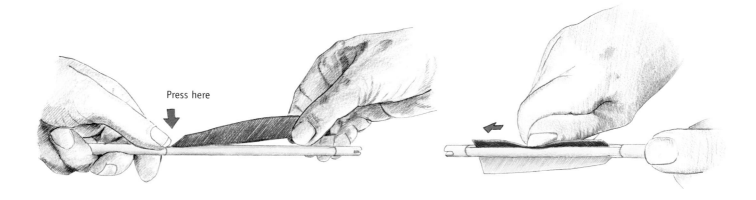

Press here

You have to be careful when gluing on the vanes: Once the two glue surfaces have been joined there is no way back.

Start with the cock feather and glue it onto the line that is perpendicular to the string notch. Hold the vane with the front end of the marking line to the shaft and press down lightly, as shown above.

Now align the entire feather along the line and push down lightly, so it can no longer slip.

Once all three feathers are in position, press them tightly against the shaft. This works best with your fingernail, as shown above.

If the feather rays get bent in the process, it doesn't matter. Just don't push so hard that they break off. Brush with your fingernail over the feather from front to back with solid pressure. It's not the duration that is important, but the strength.

Add some glue to the feather shaft and position the vane on the pencil line on the shaft. While the glue is drying, you should fasten the feather shaft with a few pins.

All three feathers should now be sticking to the arrow shaft at equal distance and with a slight slant. In the front and back, a piece of the feather shaft or the coil without feather rays must stick out (see sketch below).

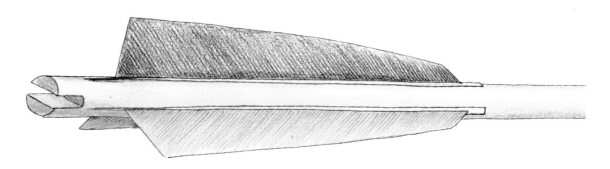

Cresting

Now provide these pieces that are sticking out with a star yarn wrap. Include the beginning in the wrap as described on page 133 and secure the end either with a double clove hitch or four half hitches (see sketch top left).

You can also finish the wrapping with tackling, which looks better and the knots of the clove hitch aren't in the way when shooting. In that case, you start wrapping at the fletching and wrap in the direction of the arrow tip.

Secure the wrapping with wood glue. Drip a few drops of glue or paste onto the wrapping and brush it around with your fingers (see sketch top center). In particular, the front wrapping is very important. If the feather quills stick away from the shaft, you can badly hurt yourself. They must be completely covered by the yarn.

If the feathers are disheveled after the gluing and wrapping, you can smooth them out very easily. Set a pot filled with a pint of water on the stove, bring to a boil, and briefly hold the back of the arrow with the feathers over the rising steam. **Only into the steam though, not the water!**

After that, you can very easily brush the feather vanes smooth again. Also, when the feathers look disheveled after you have taken a few shots, you can again fix them that way.

Before you cover the arrow with a protective layer like the bow, you can attach your ownership marks on the shaft (see sketch top right); these are also called **cresting**. Frequently they are painted on as colorful rings directly below the attachment of the feather vales. This way you can very easily distinguish your arrows from other arrows that look the same. You can also mark your arrows as the first, second, and third arrows.

This is important for some tournaments where several arrows are shot at one target and the first arrow is worth more than the other two. Of course, you can draw these color rings on with different Sharpies®, but they will be prettier if you use the proper lacquer.

Paint the rings on cleanly with a fine brush and then let everything dry well for at least a day. Then rub the entire arrow with a rag several times with milking grease. You can also rub the feathers once with the rag.

Now your arrow is finished. Together with the bow you now have everything you need for shooting. Really everything? No, a few things are still missing…

Chapter 10

Accessories

Here, we will discuss what else is needed for archery other than a bow and arrow.

When you have drawn your bow a few times in a row, the fingertips of your drawing hand are probably hurting. To prevent this, a so-called **tab** helps. It protects the fingertips from the pressure of the string when you shoot for long periods of time.

Once you have shot a few arrows, you will notice that the string tends to hit your lower left arm after the arrow leaves the bow. An **arm guard** protects against this.

Of course, you will need something to store your arrows. For this, build yourself a **quiver** or an **arrow bag**.

It's best to use goat fur. It should be nice, thin, and soft. The hair on the fur should point in one direction. You can get it at a craft store, a leather shop, a tailor's, from a goat farmer, or at a flea market. You also get the leather there.

Tab

Quiver

Arm guard

The
Tab

You will need:

- -

✓ 1 piece **flat fur**, approx. 6" x 6"
   (15 x 15cm)

✓ 1 equally large piece of **thin,
   soft leather**

✓ **Contact cement**

✓ **Hammer**

✓ **Wooden board**

✓ **Scissors**

✓ **Pencil**

✓ **Sharp knife**

- -

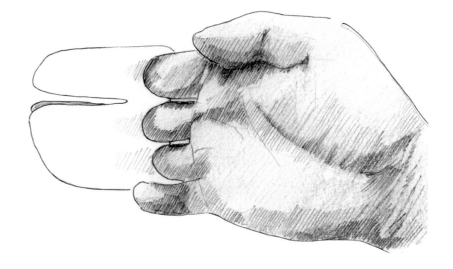

Copy the outline of the tab (top left) from the book onto a piece of paper and cut it out.

See if you can fit your fingers into the finger holes as depicted in the drawing. The tab is pushed up over the middle bones of the fingers.

The front edge of the tab should rest a little bit in front of the fingertips (see sketch at right). If the tab doesn't fit, draw a new one onto the paper that could fit.

You can also enlarge or reduce the template on the copy machine. Cut it out and check whether it fits better. Try until the tab really fits well.

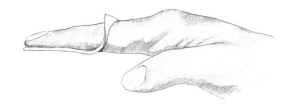

- ▷

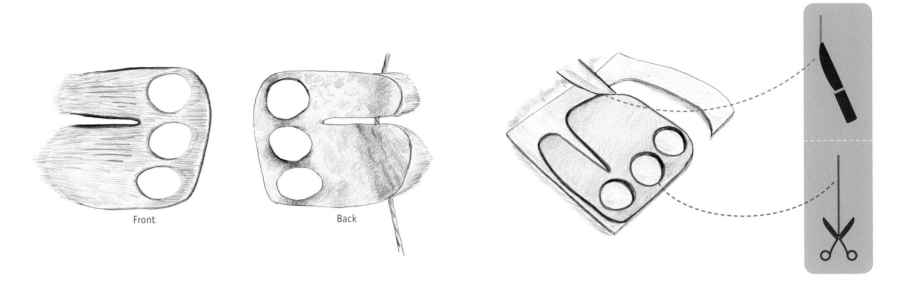

Front

Back

Now, transfer the outlines mirrored onto the **leather piece**, and in particular onto the smooth side.

Brush a thin layer of contact cement on the fur piece on the skin side and the leather piece on the rough side. Let both dry for five minutes and then hold the leather piece above the fur piece so that the slot in the tab points in the same direction as the hair on the fur (see top left). The glue surfaces must not touch though! When you have positioned the leather piece above the fur, you can glue it on.

Press down uniformly and then place the glued pieces onto the wooden board. Hit the entire surface with the dull side of the hammer — not too hard, but not too hesitant either. The pressure causes the fur and the leather to become glued together. Let the glue dry for ten minutes.

Now you can cut out the tab, but not all cuts are made with the scissors. At the front edge, the hair should remain so that the string can glide over it smoothly (see above, middle left).

Therefore, use a sharp knife to cut with in this area, but not on a board; **rather do this in the air. This works best with two people:** One holds the tab, the other cuts and pulls the piece that is supposed to be cut off away from the tab (see sketches above right). The cuts marked in red are cut with the scissors, the ones marked in green with a knife. Cut carefully — and watch your fingers.

Left-handed archers should cut out the sketch and place it on the leather face up, not mirrored.

The
Arm Guard

You can make a simple arm guard as follows. You will need:

- ✓ One piece of **thick**, **strong leather**, approx. 2" x 5" (5 x 12cm)
- ✓ **1 elastic cord**, 3/8" wide (1cm), or **leather band** 20-23" long (50-60cm)
- ✓ **Punch pliers**

You can get the leather and leather band in any leather or craft store, the elastic cord in a department store or fabric store (dry goods store), and the punch pliers in a home improvement or craft/leather store.

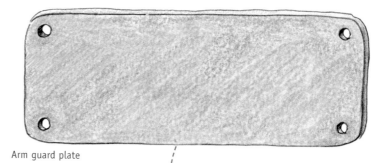

Arm guard plate

Even the archers of the Stone Age apparently had a problem with the string hitting their left arm. In many prehistoric graves, arm guards were found that generally consisted of thin stone plates. Often these plates have holes (as seen above).

If you feel like it, you can also make such an arm guard plate for yourself.

Procure an appropriate plate out of stone, bones, antlers, horn or something that you like. Drill holes into all four corners as depicted on the sketch, 1/8" (3-4mm) from the edge. Thread thin leather strands through the holes and tie the plate to your lower left arm.

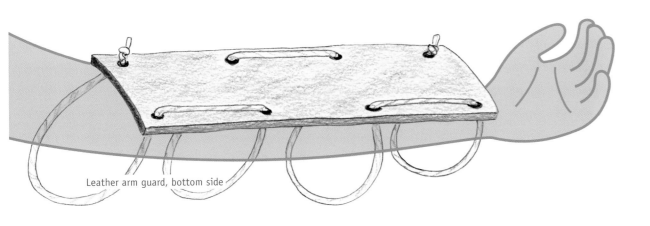

Leather arm guard, bottom side

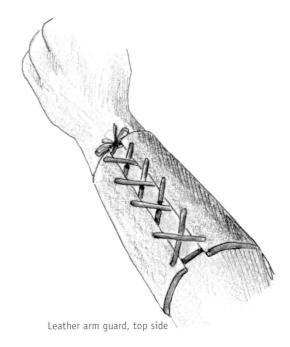

Leather arm guard, top side

For the leather arm gourd, punch four holes into the long edges of the leather piece with the punch pliers, about 1/8" (3mm) from the edge and at equal intervals. Tie a knot at the end of a piece with elastic cord and pull it through all of the holes, as depicted on the

sketch above left. Pull the cord so tight that it lies against your lower arm without pinching it, but loose enough that you can fit through it with your hand. Now tie a knot into the other end and cut off the rest.

You can also cut the leather piece wide enough to fit all the way around you lower arm. Punch holes and thread the leather band through the holes like shoelaces, as depicted on the sketch above right.

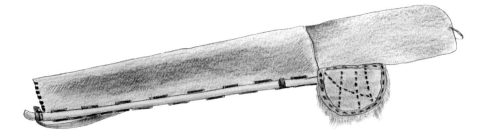

The
Quiver

You will need:

- -

✓ 1 piece strong, but not too hard **leather**, 7–8" wide (20cm) and as long as your arrows from the head to the start of the fletching

✓ 1 **Leather strand**, 1-1/4" wide (3cm), at least 4' long (1.20m)

✓ **Leather cord**, as long as possible or **thick packaging twine**

✓ **Punch pliers**

✓ **Clothespins**

✓ **Pencil**

- -

Leather and leather cords are available in leather or craft stores. You can get the punch pliers there as well or at the home improvement store.

Archeologists have only found very few remnants of quivers so far. The best preserved one is Ötzi's quiver. Its construction was very complicated, with a support stick along the side and a clap latch at the opening. However, we will be content with a simpler side quiver.

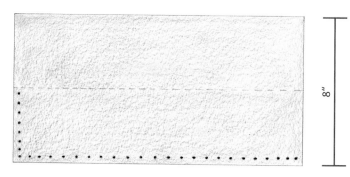

8"

Arrow length from the head to the edge of the feathering

Draw holes onto the long edge of the leather piece, at least 1/8" (4mm) from the edge and at regular intervals of 7/8" (2cm). (See sketch on right).

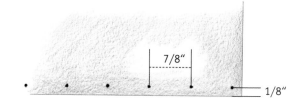

7/8"

1/8"

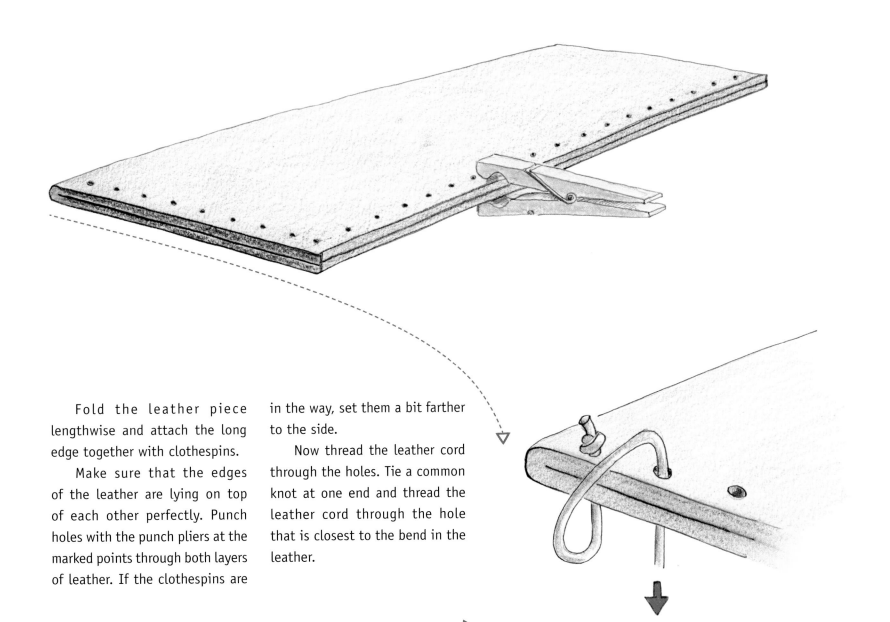

Fold the leather piece lengthwise and attach the long edge together with clothespins.

Make sure that the edges of the leather are lying on top of each other perfectly. Punch holes with the punch pliers at the marked points through both layers of leather. If the clothespins are in the way, set them a bit farther to the side.

Now thread the leather cord through the holes. Tie a common knot at one end and thread the leather cord through the hole that is closest to the bend in the leather.

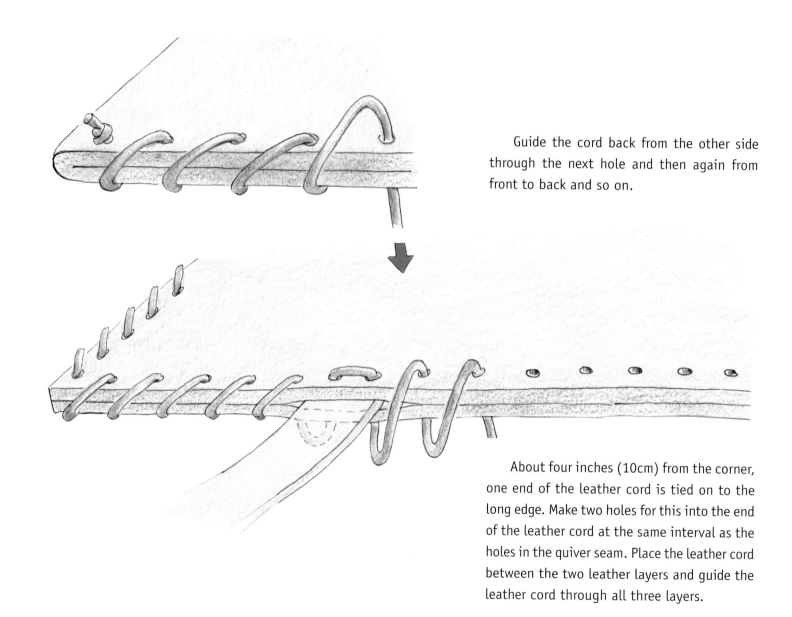

Guide the cord back from the other side through the next hole and then again from front to back and so on.

About four inches (10cm) from the corner, one end of the leather cord is tied on to the long edge. Make two holes for this into the end of the leather cord at the same interval as the holes in the quiver seam. Place the leather cord between the two leather layers and guide the leather cord through all three layers.

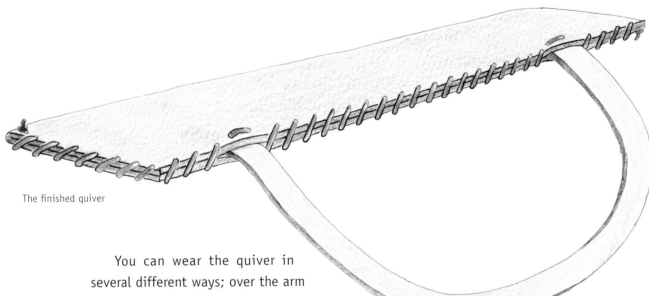

The finished quiver

Tassel

You can wear the quiver in several different ways; over the arm or over one shoulder, whichever way is most comfortable for you. Try it out and hold the loose end of the leather cord against the upper end of the quiver, about 4" (10cm) from the end of the seam.

Make sure the cord isn't twisted and mark the required length with a line on the leather. Add 1" (2cm) and then cut the cord here. Punch two holes into it and sew it into the side seam as described above. When you have reached the upper end, tie another knot.

- -

The Quiver is Done.

If you want to, you can make yourself a tassel out of many short pieces of wool yarn and tie them to the quiver. You can use the tassel to wipe the arrow tips clean if they get stuck in the ground.

Of course, you can also hold the arrows with the left hand at the bow as this Stone Age pictograph from Spain (bottom right) shows — and then you wouldn't need a quiver.

Shooting

In this chapter, you will learn how to shoot properly, why everyone shoots differently, how to avoid trouble with your uncle, and why there are ten commandments in archery as well.

Now you have your equipment ready. A large compliment for your persistence! I hope everything turned out the way you imagined. The best way to find out is by shooting with your bow.

First, though, I want to tell the story of "Harald Loudmouth": Up to now the archery tournament had been awesome. There were five in our group and we had lots of fun. The targets were placed well. The weather showed off its best side. We hiked through dense forest and green meadows all day, scored well, and felt bloody good. The evening was mild and the sky starlit. Someone played the guitar by the campfire. Someone else had brought tasty beer along.

We held back in our drinking though and went to bed in time to be fit in the morning and have a clear head. We were looking forward to a wonderful day of fun and nice shots.

The next morning we had a new addition to our group. Harald had just arrived – he wore a horned helmet, an old fur vest, black laced disco leather pants, and combat boots. "Mornin'! I am "Harald Rawpride. A warrior from the far north. I will shoot with you. Any objections?" He said and pulled a beautiful Viking bow out of his car. He put his quiver on and slammed the car door.

"Let's go, gentlemen, let us see once and for all who be the best among us!"

We looked at each other. The way Harald talked, he certainly was not from the North. And the language was probably supposed to be medieval. However, Medieval English sounds totally different. Well, alright — there were only five of us in the group, and he had to be allowed to shoot along somewhere.

In the following hours, he really got on our nerves with his warrior behavior. If one of us missed our shot, he would say "He he!" like Nelson in the television show *The Simpsons*. If he missed himself, he got very angry — cursed at his material, at the difficult targets, the weather... everything and anything. He did not shoot many points. The first time he hit, he immediately ran to the target to look at the hit. I had already strung an arrow and wanted

to shoot. Now I had to wait because of Harald and got annoyed.

Real archers only run to the target when everyone else has also shot their arrows. Otherwise, it gets dangerous. We told him so. Now he was offended and only rarely walked along up to the target. He didn't help look for arrows either when someone had missed.

During the lunch break, he disappeared in the beverage tent and reappeared with a strong odor of alcohol. Where did he come by that beautiful bow? I asked him. He deflected: "Well, we in the North know how to do it!" I was certain though that he had not built this bow himself. In the spot where the bow builder carves his sign into a bow that he built, the varnish was gone and the wood had been sanded down. None of my business ... What a braggart!

In the afternoon, Harald "Rawpride" got miserly when counting points. When nobody looked, he bent one of his arrows aside so he just scraped the next ring. That was an added point after all. I had watched him out of the corner of my eye. If someone has to cheat... Well, with his point count, he would end up in the bottom third anyhow.

This slowly began to dawn on Harald as well. To let out his frustration, he drank even more beer. Tumbled over the tournament field and shot arbitrarily at any target. Without caring whether others were still shooting. We had had enough.

We confronted him. We wanted to know why he was acting like a complete idiot here. "Because I am a great warrior! And all of you just do-nothings. I will show you how to shoot a bow!" He put an arrow on the string and shot it vertically into the air.

Even before the arrow came back down, we had grabbed Harald and pushed him with gentle determination to the exit. When we arrived at his car, we all laughed out loud. His high arrow could have been dangerous to all of us, but luckily it had not done much damage. It had — oh wonderful miracle! — flown to the parking lot and stuck in the roof of Harald's car.

It had served him right. Someone climbed up and pulled out the arrow. He broke it down the middle, pressed both halves into Harald's hand and said: "Harald Loudmouth or whatever your name is: **Bye**!!"

Sunday turned into a very nice day after all that. Harald from the high North was never again seen at this tournament.

Naturally, the story did not happen that way, but I have met guys like Harald at tournaments. Not only can they ruin your good mood, but they can also endanger themselves and others.

I built all of these "Haralds" into the short story so that you know how **NOT** to do it.

I don't want to ruin your fun with this by preaching a sermon or ridiculing someone. "Harald" probably only wanted to have fun too, but he didn't know how to behave.

10 Golden Rules

Archers carry a weapon around. If you want to participate in sports with this weapon, then you have to avoid everything that could hurt people or things. If you don't follow that rule, you very quickly find yourself in trouble. Therefore, you should obey these ten basic rules at all times. If you take these rules to heart, you won't make many mistakes.

1. COMMANDMENT

When you place an arrow on the string, it points at the target and nowhere else.

2. COMMANDMENT

Never shoot at humans or animals.

6. COMMANDMENT

Never shoot straight up into the air.

7. COMMANDMENT

Never run to the target before all other archers have shot all of their arrows.

3. COMMANDMENT

Only shoot when you have a clear head and feel well.

4. COMMANDMENT

Only shoot at long distances where you can completely overlook an area of at least 220 yards (200m) in length and width.

5. COMMANDMENT

Never shoot in the proximity of walking paths, hedges or trees, houses, streets or especially playgrounds.

8. COMMANDMENT

Check all of your equipment for damage after each shot.

9. COMMANDMENT

If you shoot outdoors, take nothing but your memories, and leave nothing but your footprints.

10. COMMANDMENT

Behave fairly and honestly at tournaments and be willing to help. Help others to follow these rules.

NOW YOU CAN GO SHOOT. OKAY, BUT WHERE?

If you live in the country, it is a bit easier:

Select a beautiful spot that you can overlook completely. The best location is at a hillside where you can find your arrows more easily. A dip or gravel pit are also good areas for catching arrows.

You live in the city?

If you have a garden and wish to shoot there, you need an arrow trap**. The garden fence will not catch the arrows since they would fly right through it. An old rug or an old piece of carpet, hung behind your target, offers more safety.

However, there should not be a walkway or parking lot behind it since as a beginner you won't even hit the carpet.

It's best if you can face your target in the direction of a fixed wall, garage, barn or similar, of course, you have to ask for permission first.

Safe is safe — at the club

If none of this is possible, look on the Internet or in the telephone book for an archery club. Many shooting athlete clubs also have an archer division with an outside range.

There, you can try your self-made bow in the safest manner, get good tips for your shooting, and perhaps meet other bow builders.

** Arrow trap nets and targets can be purchased at specialty stores.
They would be ideal as a Christmas gift.
However, in this book we want to describe how you can build everything yourself.

THE TARGET

As a target, you can use a piece of foam rubber, a sack of hay, or stick a few pieces of cardboard together with tape and draw a target on it.

Now, walk back ten steps from your target. String your bow. Be sure to relax while standing.

Also make sure that nobody is standing behind you. If the bow breaks while being drawn, the splinters fly backward!

Once my yew bow broke at full draw. One of the limbs made a large dent in the tailgate of my car. The other one left me with a scar on my head as an ever present reminder.

As a **RIGHT-HANDED ARCHER**, stand with your body at a ninety-degree to the target, your left arm pointing at the target. The left hand holds the bow, the right hand pulls the string.

Relax your body.

✓ Your feet should be approx. 10–12" apart, your upper body extended straight.

✓ Place an arrow on the string – under the nocking point, on the left side of the bow – and grasp the bowstring with the right hand, the arrow nock between your pointer and middle fingers.

✓ Breathe once and lift the bow while breathing.

✓ Hold it slightly angled to the right so that the arrow doesn't fall off.

✓ The arms and shoulders should form a straight line.

✓ Breathe out and at the same time draw the bowstring toward you with the right arm until you feel the base of your thumb in your face. This is called "anchoring."

Right-handed

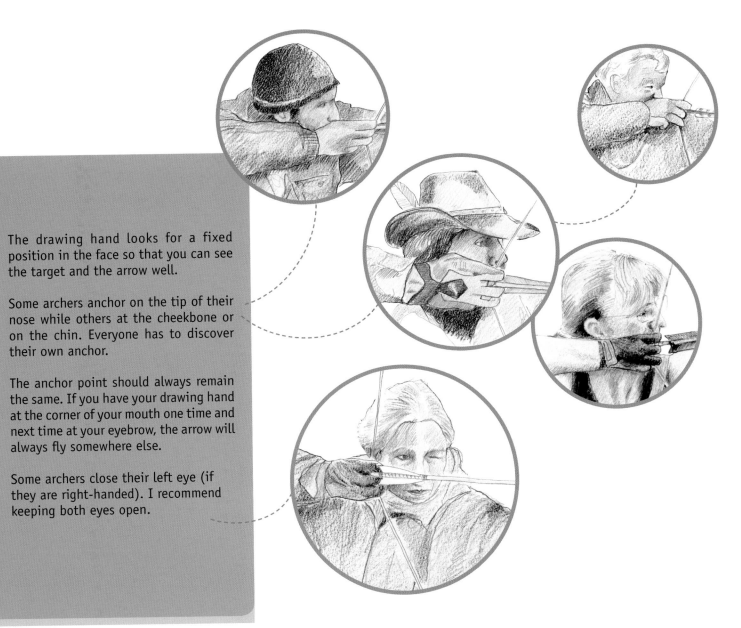

- ✓ The drawing hand looks for a fixed position in the face so that you can see the target and the arrow well.

- ✓ Some archers anchor on the tip of their nose while others at the cheekbone or on the chin. Everyone has to discover their own anchor.

- ✓ The anchor point should always remain the same. If you have your drawing hand at the corner of your mouth one time and next time at your eyebrow, the arrow will always fly somewhere else.

- ✓ Some archers close their left eye (if they are right-handed). I recommend keeping both eyes open.

1

Left-handed

2

Relax your body.

✓ Your feet should be app. ten to twelve inches apart; upper body is extended straight

✓ Place an arrow on the string – under the nocking point, on the right side of the bow – and grasp the bowstring with the left hand, the arrow nock between your pointer finger and the middle finger.

✓ Breathe once and lift the bow while breathing.

✓ Hold it slightly angled to the left so the arrow doesn't fall off.

✓ The arms and shoulders should form a straight line.

✓ Breathe out and at the same time draw the bowstring toward you, until you feel the base of your thumb in your face.

FOR ALL ARCHERS

✓ Try to aim at the target with the tip of the arrow, and remember where the tip points.

✓ Then release the arrow.

✓ Once the arrow has flown away, don't change your position yet. Also don't lower the bow or let the other arm droop. Instead look where your arrow flew.

✓ Did the arrow hit, at least on the target? If so, then remember the placement of the bow. Apparently you are standing correctly and you aimed well.
  • If the arrow hit to the left of the target though, you have to aim further to the right next time, and the other way around.

  • If the arrow flew too high, hold the bow a bit lower next time and the other way around.
  • If the arrows are swinging up and down during flight and are always crooked in the target, your nock point isn't right.

✓ Check again whether the little knot on the string is really 1/8" to 1/4" (5mm) above the marked center of the string (see page 125), and make sure that the arrow is always placed in the center of the bow.

✓ Don't aim too long with the bow. When the bow is drawn, that stresses the cells in the wood. It is said that when a bow is fully drawn, it is 7/8 broken!

Therefore:
Lift the bow, exhale, and draw fully... Briefly sight the target, no longer than one, two seconds — and release the arrow. A fluid motion.

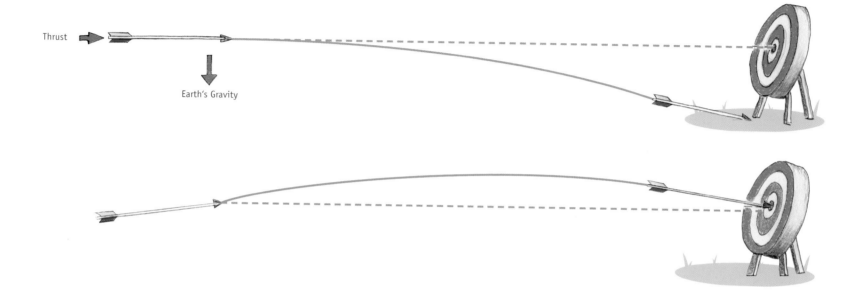

Thrust

Earth's Gravity

This is the way you practice shot upon shot until the results improve. Try to always take up the same posture and always anchor in the same point when you draw your bow back.

When you hit well at ten paces, then you can go a few yards backwards. When you shoot now, you will discover that you have to hold the bow a bit higher. The arrow is pulled downward during flight by the Earth's gravity. It never really flies straight, but rather in an arch toward the target.

The further you are from the target, the higher you have to hold the bow. However, it's better to aim too low rather than too high; otherwise, you will have to search for your arrows.

Only when all of the archers have shot their arrows do they approach the target together. You should cautiously advance and watch for arrows that are sticking flat in the ground in front of the target. If you step on one, they break quickly.

PULLING ARROWS

For the arrows that are stuck in the target, you should always grab them in the front and pull them out backwards. Make sure that no one is standing behind you — quite a few have found themselves suddenly with a knock in the nose when pulling arrows. That can blow up in your face too!

If an arrow is stuck in the target past the feathers, then you have to pull it out toward the back. If you pull it from the front, the feathers will tear off the shaft. Perhaps you should build a sturdier target at that point.

Once everyone has found their arrows, the next round can begin. Verify first that nobody is looking for arrows behind the target anymore!

AFTER TAKING YOUR SHOT

Each time you shoot, you should check your equipment. Is the string still intact? Did the bow tear or bend? Are the arrow shafts damaged? Sometimes breaks hide under the wrappings. Cautiously bend the arrows: Are they still okay?

I had to watch once as someone shot an arrow into his own hand. He didn't notice a hidden break on a shaft. The arrow broke in two when he shot and the fletched end drove deep into his left hand. That hurt like the devil and he had to go to the hospital.

Also: Only when everything has been checked do you pack up your gear. The bow should be unstrung after shooting and stored that way.

You should never leave a bow strung longer than necessary. The wood cells will thank you. Store the equipment in your room, but not directly by or above the heater. The bow could dry out, become brittle, and break.

Make sure the bow remains out of the reach of little siblings. As you know, it is not a toy.

To prevent from getting bored there are many possibilities for new self-made targets. For example try a bow memory, bow dart, or homemade three-dimensional animals.

You don't have to only shoot at targets with your bow. You can have a long-distance shooting competition with your friends, but you will need a lot of room for this and a clear view.

Roving or clout shooting is also fun. Here the goal is to shoot the arrow at a large unknown distance into the proximity of a flag that is sticking out of the ground. It's like playing golf with a bow.

At a distance of about 220 yards (200m), place a flag or a stick into the meadow and try to get as close as possible with as few shots as possible. The one who needed the fewest shots wins — or the one who gets closest to the flag with a specific number of shots wins.

Chapter 12:

Appendix

Glossary
and Closing Remarks

What is what?

Alamanni:	Germanic tribe, the term probably stems from "all men"
Anchor point:	Spot in the archer's face where the drawing hand always rests when shooting
Annual ring:	Every year a tree gets thicker by one ring of wood cells. Annual rings are concentric around the pith.
Arquebus:	Medieval firearm
Aurochs:	Extinct cattle species
Back of the bow:	Points away from the archer
Belly of the bow:	Points at the archer
Bow feather:	Front, small side of the feather
Bow hand:	Holds the bow
Bowline knot:	Sailor's knot, to tie an easily undone loop
Circumvallation:	When a tree is injured, it forms a bulge out of wood cells around the wound.

Clout shooting:	Shooting at a long-distance target
Clove hitch:	Sailor's knot for attaching a rope to the mast
Cock feather:	Stands perpendicular to the string notch and has a different color than the other feathers
Concave:	Bent toward the inside
Convex:	Bent toward the outside
Cresting:	Property marks, color rings on the shaft of an arrow
Cross-cut section:	When you saw a tree or a board, the cutting surfaces are the cross-cut sections.
Deflexive:	Bent toward the archer
Draw:	The distance that you can draw a bow
Draw hand:	Pulls the string toward the archer
Ear:	Loop
Fiberglass bow:	Modern sports bow made of laminated thin wood boards and a layer of resin, strengthened with fiberglass on both sides.
Fluflu:	Arrow with a lot of fletching for hunting birds
Half hitch:	Loop in a rope or a string, two half hitches = one clove hitch

Holmegaard:	Middle Stone Age type of bow, named after a moor on Zealand (Denmark)
Homo erectus:	From the Latin *Homo* = human and *erectus* = upright. Very prehistoric type of people, belong to our ancestors
Homo sapiens:	Modern humans
Loop:	Loop at the end of the string, also called ear
Mesolithic:	Middle Stone Age (from the Greek *meso* = middle, *lithos* = stone), approx. 10,000–7,500 before today
Microlith:	Small flint tip (from the Greek *mikros* = small, *lithos* = stone)
Musket:	Medieval firearm
Neanderthal:	Prehistoric type of people, lived in Europe prior to the modern human
Neolithic:	New Stone Age (from the Greek *neos* = new, *lithos* = stone), approx. 7,500–5,000 before today
Nock:	Back end of the arrow with the string notch
Nocking point:	This is where the arrow is placed on the string.
Paleolithic:	Old Stone Age, from the beginnings of humanity until approx. 10,000 before today

Periderm:	The outermost layer of a tree.
Pith:	Pipe in the center of the tree trunk, serves to transport nutrients in the young plant
Reflexive:	Bent away from the archer
Release:	Moment in which the string is let go
Roving:	Shooting at targets at different long distances
Sight:	Device for aiming precisely at the target
Stabilizers:	Rods with weights at the end that are screwed onto the back of the bow in modern bows. They cause the bow to shoot calmer.
Tab:	Finger protection for the draw hand
Tackling:	Protective wrapping around a rope (sailor language)
Tail:	Back part
Tiller:	Fine control for the bendability of a bow
Tiller stick:	Serves to control the curvature of the bow
Tip:	Tip of a limb

At the End

I have described in this book how I build bows and arrows and how I shoot. Much of it I discovered myself through experimentation while some I learned from others.

There are many different ways to build bows and even more ways to shoot them. Therefore, this book is only meant as a foundation.

When you meet other people who also do archery, look closely and listen carefully: They probably know things I don't or have tips on how you can improve your skills even more. You don't always have to listen to everything others say, but sometimes it is worth it. You never stop learning.

If someone claims to know it all and that his style of shooting is the best, then he hasn't understood anything.

However, if you follow the tips and rules in this book, you will enjoy your bow for a long time. Perhaps we will meet someday at a tournament and you can tell me how you fared while building your bow and shooting it.

I am always grateful for suggestions and criticism regarding this book as well. You can reach me via my website:

www.archaeo-technik.de

I wish you a lot of fun with your bow.

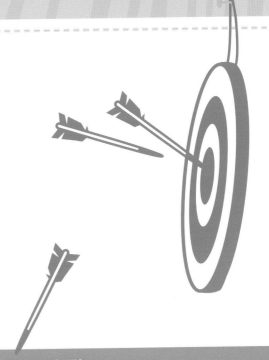

MAY YOUR ARROW ALWAYS HIT ITS TARGET!

About the Author

Wulf Hein first learned to be a professional carpenter. Since he had been interested in history and archeology since his school days, he specialized in the reconstruction of historic artifacts. For over twenty years now, he has been an expert in the area of experimental archeology and archeo-technology.

Whether digging out Ötzi's fur clothing or a Neolithic village, Wulf has rebuilt and helped reconstruct many small and large objects, mostly for museums and exhibitions. However, you can also see his work in movies and television productions.

Since he himself has so much fun "re-crafting," which he hopes to pass on to children in particular, Wulf developed instructional material for the Stone Age, the Roman times, and the Middle Ages.

And that is why he finally wrote this book specifically for YOU.